HOLY HOOK UP: EQUIPPING LEADERS TO LEAD OTHERS, A LEADERSHIP PARADIGM FOR THE TWENTY FIRST CENTRY

Reginald L. Dawkins

B.A., North Greenville University, 2000
MDiv., Interdenominational Theological Center and Morehouse School of Religion, 2004
DMin., United Theological Seminary, 2009

dpRochelle
PO Box 9523
Hampton, Virginia 23670
1 (757) 825-0030
ItsmeDrIFP.org

© *2017 Reginald L. Dawkins. All Rights Reserved*

No part of this book may be reproduced, stored in a retrieval system, or transmitted by any means without the written permission of the author.

First published by dpRochelle 2/28/17

Edited by Dr. Reginald L. Dawkins

ISBN: 978-0-9862389-9-4

Printed in the United States of America, Hampton, VA

Acknowledgements

I would like to thank God for helping me to write this book to help leaders and believers in the Christian faith. My wife, Alethia, for her love, support and encouragement during this process. My sisters, Renee and Angie, for their prayers and encouragement. Dr. Tony Boyce, Dr. Keith Tillett and Dr. Steve Lomax for doing the forward and reviews.

Triumph Christian Center church family for your prayers and support that you have given me during this phase in my ministry. Latonya Hughes for giving me the advice and avenue to make this happen. A special thank you to Tiara Williams, my assistant, for typing the manuscript.

To all my sons and daughters in the ministry, I hope this book will help you to develop as strong leaders in the Christian Faith.

I dedicated this book to my nephews, Jaylen and Trey, as a seed for what you will do in the future…

CONTENTS

i	Foreword	
iii	Reviews	
v	Introduction	
1	Chapter I	My Personal Connection with the Holy
15	Chapter II	God, The "Holy" Liberator
59	Chapter III	The "Holy" Connection in the Old Testament
81	Chapter IV	The "Holy" Connection in the New Testament
99	Chapter V	The "Holy" Connection
133	Chapter VI	The "Holy" Connection in an Urban Setting
145	Chapter VII	The Conclusion
149	Answer Key	
159	Notes	

FOREWORD

By Dr. Tony Boyce[1]

How do pastors and church leaders provide practical models and messages for ministry to our hurting congregations and communities? The Holy Hook Up provides relevant answers to this question through the interpretive lens of liberation theology. Liberation theology proposes that God is on the side of the oppressed, yet we seem to be lacking the volume and veracity of churches that are proclaiming the truth of God's liberation of oppressed persons. The 21st century church must provide relevant ministries and models to address the mythology of a post racial America, police brutality, poverty, and crime just to name a few crises that face the church. God's church serves as the ambassador of the power of liberation, however we need practical guidance on reaching that expected end. The end we seek must not only be theologically sound, but also culturally relevant. The Holy Hookup will provide readers with the direction and inspiration that are needed to reach our leaders, churches, and communities at their time of need. We need a message, a model, and a mission for liberation. The time is now to experience God's liberation. Let us make the Holy Hook Up!

---

[1] Tony Boyce, D.Min. is the pastor of Mt. Emmanuel Missionary Baptist Church in Greenville, SC. He received his BS degree in Elementary Education, M.Div. from the Interdenominational Theological Center, and Doctor of Ministry Degree from Gardner-Webb University. He is considered a proven expert in conflict resolution, church administration, and community missions on the local and national convention levels.

REVIEWS

Dr. Reginald Dawkins, one of Greenville, South Carolina's brightest, is extremely serious and profoundly committed to the overall work of ministry. I had the privilege of meeting Dr. Dawkins in Dayton, Ohio, as we both entered the Doctor of Ministry degree program in 2006 at United Theological Seminary. For the many years I have known him, his actions have evidenced his heartfelt dedication to the work of ministry. His level of genuineness and commitment is found in his clarion call and his willingness to maximize that call in every faucet of ministry from his preparation through academic achievement to his faithfulness to the church he founded: Triumph Christian Center in Newport News, VA. From the daily work of the pastorate to the writing of his book, *"The Holy Hook Up"* Dr. Dawkins' dedication exudes through his ministry and his book as it speaks directly to the hearts and minds of the churched and unchurched.

When Dr. Dawkins asked me if I would be willing to write a review for his book, it took me only a second to say yes, because, *"The Holy Hook Up"* speaks to a prevalent problem in the 21st century; the problem of ineffective and inefficient leadership. Leadership has become stagnant and stale in many places but Dr. Dawkins book will revitalize leadership by helping to equip leaders to lead others in the 21st century. This transformative book is a much needed source and will also help church leaders become spiritually accountable and effective as liberation theology becomes the very core of their spiritual understanding. It reveals to leadership that they must keep liberation theology at the heart of the Christian experience as it seeks to utilize the Exodus narrative to validate that liberation theology is a part of God's plan. Finally, it demonstrates that God is a God of justice seeking to liberate those who are the least, the last and the left-out. This book has certainly been a tremendous blessing to me and I am more than confident that *"The Holy Hook Up"* will bless both lay and clergy alike who wish to methodically delve into it.

Much thanks to you, Dr. Dawkins. *The Holy Hook Up* will make a difference.

Dr. Keith D. Tillett, B.A., M. Div., D. Min.
Pastor: St. Paul A.M.E. Zion Church
Ewing, New Jersey
November 2015

Reverend Dr. Stephen Lomax
Five time author, teacher and pastor

My friend and brother in Christ, Dr. Reginald Dawkins has written a very important educational and inspirational work. He has taken a spiritually exegetical look at how God hooks up with people willing to be used by Him.

Each chapter reveals some aspect of how hooking up with the Holiness of God leads to liberation and wholeness. For instance, chapter one reveals how hooking up with God brought tremendous blessings to the author through liberation theology. A chapter full of encouragement and inspiration. Thus, if you miss reading this great piece of work, you will miss a theological Rembrandt.

INTRODUCTION

This book will take a look at how God hooks up with the person who is open for His guidance. This book is derived from my Doctoral Ministry project with United Theological Seminary. It shows how leaders can lead others into a paradigm of change for the twenty-first century. It is a practical and easy read for all ages.

Each chapter is designed to show how hooking up with the Holy can lead to liberation and wholeness. Chapter one deals with my personal encounter with the Holy. It gives a brief history of my conversion story, call to ministry, and how my values were shaped in dealing with the Holy. Chapter two deals with how God brings about liberation to His people; the central point is that God uses a process to liberate His people and elects people who feel insufficient. In addition, chapter two shows how Jesus was a proponent of liberation throughout the Gospels as he dealt with people who were oppressed, marginalized, and considered outcasts. Also, the Holy is calling us to bring about human liberation in the lives of those who feel marginalized in the world in which we live.

Chapter three deals with the Holy Hook-Up in the Old Testament. It takes a fresh look at how leaders who take the role of leadership must be relevant and concerned about God's intervention in the lives of those He loves. He uses Moses as His Old Testament model for pastoral leadership by using the qualities and characteristics that made Moses a perfect model for leaders to follow. Moses was commissioned by God, courageous to confront his many challenges, committed to God, and confident that God would establish his leadership. It is a perfect model for pastoral leadership.

Chapter four looks at the Holy Hook-Up in the New Testament. It takes a look at the New Testament model that Jesus demonstrated as a leader. Jesus achieved His missions by preaching, teaching, healing, and giving of Himself. I explored each of these principles that exemplified Jesus as a great model and example for others to follow. In order for the church to become an agent of change, it must take on the characteristics, style, and exemplary life that Jesus lived, talked, and demonstrated.

Chapter five deals with the Holy Hook-Up of church fathers and leaders historically. Historically leadership training was important for leaders to develop and maintain a level of keeping leaders on task and relevant for their particular church. Origen, Augustine, Martin

Luther, Martin Luther King, Jr., and other church fathers will help readers to understand leadership from a historical perspective. This chapter will examine leadership by examining two principles: how biblical leaders use effective administrative skills to bring about change, and how to be equipped to manage conflict that can arise during change.

Chapter six deals with the Holy Hook-Up in an urban setting. This chapter deals with the research that was done on an urban church in Newport News, Virginia. It talks about the hypothesis of how you can take twelve key leaders to bring about training, teaching, and preaching that will be effective in bringing about transformation. This chapter deals with the project that was designed, implemented, and tested at an urban church in Virginia. It shows how to deal with conflict resolution that is brought on by change that happens in a local church. It helps the reader to understand the basic administrative skills in leading a ministry, their weaknesses and strengths in ministry, their attitude about change, their particular style of leadership, how to handle conflict management, and the difference between interpersonal conflict and situational conflict. It is the nuts and bolts of putting it into practice.

HOLY HOOK UP: EQUIPPING LEADERS TO LEAD OTHERS, A LEADERSHIP PARADIGM FOR THE TWENTY FIRST CENTRY

Reginald L. Dawkins

B.A., North Greenville University, 2000
MDiv., Interdenominational Theological Center and
Morehouse School of Religion, 2004
DMin., United Theological Seminary, 2009

CHAPTER I

MY PERSONAL CONNECTION WITH THE "HOLY"

MY CONVERSION STORY

I was around the church all my life. It was during this time that I lived a crazy and foolish life. My life was unfulfilling and unrewarding. I sang on the choir and participated in the youth groups but I was not saved. There was a void in my life and I realized that I needed Christ. One Thursday night when I was thirteen I trusted Christ as my personal Savior during the revival. I asked Christ to save me and cleanse me of all of my sin and He did it that day. I have trusted Him since that day. Before I grew in the knowledge of the Lord, I asked the Lord to save me a couple of times.

During my adolescent and teenage years, I went to a fire baptized holiness school that taught that you could lose your salvation at any time. This experience was helpful and scary at the same time. Helpful in the sense that it taught me the importance of reading and learning the scriptures. It was scary because I believed that I could lose my salvation. Every time there was an altar call, I would go up and get right with God. I was and still am amazed at the pressure that it put on the follower in the movement. The women were not allowed to wear makeup or pants. They were missionaries who could not preach or have any authority over a man. It was a strict religious tyranny.

CALL TO THE MINISTRY

I was called into the ministry when I was a young man. Like Jeremiah, my call was without repentance. I didn't hear voices, see lighting flashing or hear thunder rolling. However, there was a burning within me to preach the gospel.

When I was growing up and even now, I preach to everything and everybody. I recall as a young man preaching in the ghetto to perfect strangers. I would walk to my auntie's house from school, stand on the corner and preach to cars passing by, dogs, cats, insects, buses, drunks, and anybody who would listen. I was not afraid of being shot, beaten, or laughed at; I had a word shut up in my bones that I had to get it out. My brother, sisters and neighbors would let me preach to them after church every Sunday. I also had a short revival with them during the week. I would stand on the wall and preach to them and come down and curse them out.

I shared with my pastor when I was fourteen years

old that God was calling me into the ministry. He told me to read the entire Bible and come back. When I finished reading the entire Bible a year later, I shared with him that I still had the burning to preach. He told me to read it again. I guessed he wanted me to be sure. During this time, my father died of liver disease from drinking too much alcohol. It was a sad time in my life. My father and I were very close. In the midst of his death, the calling to preach became even stronger.

    We started attending a church that was closer to home. I shared with my new pastor the call that God had on my life and he confirmed it by licensing me into the ministry and becoming my mentor. As a young preacher, I had an opportunity to follow and learn from my mentor who became like a father figure in my life. He was an outgoing person who loved life to the fullest. He shared with me the do's and don'ts for ministry. As I watched him go through some major storms as a pastor, I would often pick him up and we would ride around discussing the dark side of the ministry. He told me the people he gave the most to, turned their backs on him and fought him at the same time. He would tell me often, "don't get too close to the members, they will hurt you." I have often wondered if that is why I am sometimes afraid of getting too close to some of the members. As I watched him lead our church, I picked up some of his pastoral strengths and weaknesses. He encouraged me to go to school to further my theological education for the ministry. He left the church to start a ministry in Atlanta, Ga.

After he left, there was a group that wanted me to become pastor, but I was contemplating moving to Indianapolis to live with my mother whose job moved her to that city. I declined that opportunity to serve my home church. After much prayer, I decided not to go to Indianapolis and six month later St. Matthew Baptist Church called me to be their pastor.

HOW MY VALUES WERE SHAPED

I believe my values were shaped by personal relationships, work experiences, and intellectual developments. I learned the value of listening to the voice of the Holy Spirit.

I worked as a chaplain at the Greenville Memorial Hospital and pastored St. Matthew Baptist Church at the same time. It was during this time that I learned to listen to the voice of the Holy Spirit. When I visited the hospital room of patients, they had questions that I could not answer and conditions that were unexplainable. When I started clinical pastoral education, I thought I had all the answers. Over a period of time and through clinical verbatim I learned that we all have issues and I don't have the answers to fix the world. I recall working one night when I received a call to counsel a young man who had received word that his future wife had been killed. I was full of anxiety and fear because I did not know what to say. When I open the door to the emergency waiting room, there stood a white guy with a rebel shirt, and with a chain hanging from his side. He had long hair that smelled like old rags and cowboy boots that appeared to be covered with dirt and blood. I informed him that I was the chaplain and that I received a call concerning his fiancée. He started to cry and I placed my hand on his shoulder and I did not say a word. He started to share with me that he and his fiancée had a fight the other day and they had not reconciled. He continued verbalizing his many regrets and frustrations. After sitting with him for an hour, just listening, his family arrived and I slowly walked away and he said, "Chap, thanks for everything." As I reflect on that experience, I recall that I didn't say anything; I just sat with him in his pain. I learned that the ministry of presence is so powerful. In the midst of our pain, God is yet speaking.

During my intellectual development, I was affirmed by my professors, peers, and persons in whom I came in contact with. I learned a lot in the classroom as well as from the outside of the classroom. When I was in high school, a counselor told my mother and father that I could not learn because I had a learning disability. She said, "The best thing that Reggie can do is get a job and hope for the best." My mother did not send me (Pay for) to school like my brother and sisters. She told me to go to work. It was after I started preaching that I realized that I needed an education to strengthen my intellectual development in order to strengthen the people that God had entrusted to me. My wife encouraged me to go back to school and pursue an undergraduate degree and I did. I was not going to seminary because I was under the impression that an undergraduate degree was sufficient. I visited the Morehouse School of Religion at the Interdenominational Theological Center with a friend who was interested in attending the school but I was not. He told me to pick up some information in the event that I changed my mind in the future. I brought the information back home and shared it with my wife and she said emphatically, "You can do that!" She gave me the affirmation to pursue another degree. In my mind I wondered if I could really do it—I have a history with the master, but I knew that God brought me through North Greenville University in spite of the odds. While at Morehouse School of Religion, I was liberated from my biases against women in ministry and other "isms" that are outdated and outrageous. I have changed intellectually in many positive ways. Now when I approach any given task, I have learned how to be more critical concerning the author, the background, the environment, and his intentions for writing certain material. Seminary has taught me how to be a critical thinker and has challenged and stretched my belief system beyond my greatest imagination.

Kushner in his book *Living a Life that Matters* points out that "we all know the feeling of being in the supporting actor in other people's movies, not being in the spotlight but doing things that shape and drive the plot."[2] If you really think about it, all of us are supporting actors to someone or another. I feel like I am a supporting actor to my sons in the ministry. For example, one Saturday one son in the ministry and I worked on a project together that really stressed both of us out. He was asked by a church which he was running for the office of pastor to present

---

[2] Harold S. Kushner, *Living a Life that Matters* (Anchor Books A Division of Random House, Inc., New York, 2001), 126.

them with a proposal for salary, no information was given. Before we met, I had him to call the church to get some information concerning their budget and financial information but they refused to give any information concerning their financial standing. I had never heard of or experienced anything like this before. We had been talking about the importance of being a good leader and presenting ourselves in a fashion that would help and aid the overall ministry. But I must confess that I wanted him to tell the church in which he was running for candidacy to forget it, but I didn't. I have come to realize that every church is not on the same level. I helped him put together a package that addressed three different levels that the church could have been on during the time they were without a Pastor. We also included an article concerning pastoral compensations and benefits for the search committee. We gave them more than what they asked for. I had him address where he thought the church was (based on persons he would see on Sunday morning and information he received through the grapevine) and the compensation that he felt that the church could pay based on his information. I felt like I was his supporting actor in helping him pull this together. I did not mention my name and asked him to do the same. I was supporting him from behind the scenes. There are many more people that I can think of that I may have helped without saying a word. The Bible says "all that you do, do as unto the Lord." I try to do what I can as though I am doing it unto the Lord. I realize that people will take you for granted and assume that you have to do what you do, but you don't. I believe that God is calling all of us to a higher standard in terms of helping others as they go through their ups and downs. I believe that we all are supporting actors in someone's life. It may be small or great but we are there to make an impact in their lives.

Spiritually, I have grown to new and higher levels in my faith and commitment to the Lord. I have a new outlook on God. I have learned to appreciate the small things that God does for me daily. It amazes me how a God so large and so great can love a person like me. As I listen to the professors and my colleagues, I am amazed at the work that God is doing in the lives of other people as well. I feel that Morehouse School of Religion has helped me to grow to higher levels in my commitment to Christ and His work. I have a deeper understanding concerning God. I am trying to keep God out of the box that I had God in when I enrolled. I view my spiritual walk with God as an unfolding experience that I am learning more and more about every day.

CHAPTER 1 – YOUR PERSONAL CONNECTION WITH THE "HOLY."

Discussion Questions

1. Explain your personal connection with the "Holy."

    _____
    _____
    _____
    _____
    _____
    _____

2. What is it that the "Holy" is calling you to do?

    _____
    _____
    _____
    _____
    _____
    _____

3. Do you have a passion to do what the "Holy" is calling you to do?

    _____
    _____
    _____
    _____
    _____
    _____

4. How are your values shaped around your calling?

   _____
   _____
   _____
   _____
   _____
   _____
   _____

5. What is leadership?

   _____
   _____
   _____
   _____
   _____
   _____
   _____

6. Who helped shape your view of leadership?

   _____
   _____
   _____
   _____
   _____
   _____
   _____

7. Name five Biblical models of leadership.

___

8. Name five secular models of leadership.

___

9. How important is it to have someone to help the leader achieve his or her goal?

___

10. Do you think it is important for leaders to listen to the voice of the Holy Spirit? If so, why?

_____
_____
_____
_____
_____
_____

11. Write your spiritual journey. Detail how your journey and calling has helped you to discern the will of God in your life.

_____
_____
_____
_____
_____
_____
_____
_____
_____
_____
_____
_____
_____
_____
_____
_____
_____
_____

CHAPTER II

GOD, THE "HOLY" LIBERATOR

If church leaders [at this institution] are to be transformed into spiritually responsible and impactful individuals, a theology of liberation must be the foundation of this God-mandated experience because it will show them how God is liberating His people. Church leaders must believe not only in the biblical and practical aspects of church work, but that it is ordained by God. They must have a reasonable understanding of the freedom that is inherent in liberation theology. Church leaders need to accept the fact that they, themselves, have been an oppressed people due to their inability to perceive, or bring into being, a community that espouses the concept of liberation theology. In other words, one cannot effectively deliver or produce something in which one does not believe or does not practice.

I believe that church leaders, both lay and clergy, must have a level of theological training, as presented by the pastor, that is consistent with their leadership responsibilities. Therefore, in order to assist the pastor with infusing liberation theology into the larger congregation, it is of the utmost importance that leaders, especially those who will pioneer this *leadership paradigm project*, allow themselves to not only experience the real freedom of God, through Jesus Christ and this faith community, but better understand their expanding role of exemplar in liberation theology.

First, leaders must keep in mind that liberation theology is at the center of the Christian religion. Jesus started his ministry with the words, "The Spirit of the Lord is on me, because He has anointed me to preach good news to the poor. He has sent me to proclaim freedom for the prisoners and recovery of sight for the blind, to release the oppressed, to proclaim the year of the Lord's favor."[3] Christ's messages pointed directly to liberating those who were oppressed. His whole mission was to bring about liberation. Liberation theology leads to the liberation of a people who have been oppressed by their taskmasters. James H. Cone, in *A Black Theology of Liberation,* claims, "it is a rational study of the being of God in the world in light of the existential situation of an oppressed community, relating the forces of liberation to the essence of the gospel, which is Jesus Christ."[4] I believe that this is

---

[3] *The Holy Bible : New International Version*, electronic ed. (Grand Rapids: Zondervan, 1996, c1984), Lk 4:18-19.
[4] James Cone, *A Black Theology Of Liberation* (Maryknoll, NY: Orbis Books, 1990), 1.

the central mark of leadership in this community. It is indeed a theology that focuses on the liberation of the oppressed.

I believe that leaders must have a sense of liberation for those who are oppressed. The sole reason for Christian Theology to exist, according to Cone, "is to put into ordered speech the meaning of God's activity in the world, so that the community of the oppressed will recognize that its inner thrust for liberation is not only consistent with the gospel, but is the gospel of Jesus Christ."[5] There can be no good Christian theology if it is not connected with the downcast and underprivileged. God was about liberating those who were on the bottom of the social order.

Secondly, leaders must keep in mind that the exodus was a part of God's liberation plan. When looking at the Exodus sojourn, readers must keep in mind that Moses was not only a great leader but he was a liberator. God was leading him to bring about liberation in the lives of the Israelites. Scholars have similar assessments concerning the Exodus sojourn and it significance to liberation. J. Deotis Roberts asserts that:

---

[5] Ibid.

The 'Exodus Paradigm' is, for Cone, the exegetical perspective for understanding God's liberating message for the oppressed. It is also a clue for understanding the Old Testament, because biblical interpretation for Cone is grounded Christological. The Exodus motif is reinforced by the Lukan text (Luke 4:18-19), which describes Jesus' sense of mission, the 'liberation' of humankind. Cone writes that 'if the history of Israel and the New Testament description of the historical Jesus reveal that God is a God who is identified with Israel because it is an oppressed community, the resurrection of Jesus means that all oppressed peoples become his people. Herein lies the universal note implied in the gospel message of Jesus.[6]

I believe that the message that God exemplified through delivering His people from oppression should be the same message that church leaders exemplify when liberating the people in whom God has called them to lead. The message was a message of hope that God is moving His people to a place greater than where they have been. Richard Bondi asserts that, "Moral leadership has to do with ensuring that the direction and form of that movement allow people to discover the true destination of their

---

[6] J. Deotis Roberts, *Africentric Christianity: A Theological Appraisal For Ministry* (Valley Forge: Judson Press, 2000), 45.

restless hearts and to live that out in a world full of voices calling us to other destination."[7] If liberation is to take place, there must be people who are willing to move in the direction God is leading and accept the changes that liberation will bring.

Third, when speaking of Christian theology and liberation, I assert that the leader must realize that the exodus of the children is a perfect picture of a God who is the God of and for those who labor and are heavy burdened. Owen C. Thomas, in *Introduction to Theology*, points out that Gods activity can be traced in human history. He states, "Thus it might be expected that the most revealing area of God's activity would be human history. But why is the history of Israel more revealing of God than the history of other nations? The answer from Israel is that God has chosen Israel for this purpose so that she may become a witness to God before the nations of the world. As to why Israel was chosen rather than another nation, there is no answer except the mystery of the divine choosing."[8] I contend that the church has been chosen to do a greater work for God in the area of liberation. It is

---

[7] Terry Thomas. *An Exploration into the Task of Leadership*, lecture notes from cluster group/ Handout. 8.

[8] Owen C. Thomas and Ellen K. Wondra, *Introduction to Theology* (Harrisburg, Pennsylvania: Morehouse Publishing, 2002), 32.

important for leaders to view God as a deliverer of the people. There are people surrounding the church and in the church that need a God who can liberate them from oppression. The church must keep in mind that Israel's deliverance certainly was not because Israel had a great attitude or disposition but they had the divine favor of God. God was liberating them from their oppressor.

In conclusion, it is through liberation that God used leaders to deliver His people from the snares of being marginalized. The task of liberation is so vital, as Owen Thomas points out, "The exodus from Israel, Jesus' proclamation of the kingdom of God, and his ministry, along with his death and resurrection, are key biblical events. Liberation entails two things: the thorough transformation of oppressive socioeconomic, political, and cultural systems into systems that promote the well-being and just treatment of all persons; and the coming into full humanity and dignity of those who have been oppressed, marginalized, or subjugated. These two aspects must be achieved together; one does not precede the other."[9] I contend that it is the responsibility of the total leadership in the church to aid and assist those who are marginalized by society and give them the helping hand that they need.

---

[9] Ibid., 192.

Leadership must have a strong desire to see transformation of oppressive socioeconomic, political, and cultural systems into systems that will aid and support those who have been marginalized. Therefore, I would like to explore three aspects of liberation that will strengthen the leadership and bring about a paradigm of change. I will examine God as a liberator, Jesus as a liberator, and how human liberation is depicted throughout the Bible.

GOD AS A LIBERATOR

When one talks about theology, it is a talk about God. Joseph A. Johnson, in *Proclamation Theology,* points out that theology is "a study of God, who has made his decisive revelation in Jesus Christ, for man's salvation, liberation, and reconciliation. The God-talk of theology should not obscure one obvious fact, that it is man who speaks to God and in God-talk, man seeks to understand his relationship to that absolute reality called God."[10] It is through liberation theology that we see and sense God delivering an oppressed and disenfranchised people. If theology is to be

---

[10] Joseph A. Johnson, *Proclamation Theology* (Shreveport, Louisiana: Fourth Episcopal District Press, 1977), 132.

discussed, it must arise from the treatment that God is a liberator of the oppressed.

I will examine five central points about God bringing about liberation to His people. The central points:

(1) God uses a process to liberate them.
(2) God elected Israel to be His people.
(3) God appointed a leader by the name of Moses in spite of his insufficiency.
(4) God is at His best when liberating those who are oppressed by the hand of the oppressor.
(5) In the history of God's revealed word, the Bible indicates how very active God is advocating for the poor and less fortunate because of His love for them.

GOD USES A PROCESS TO BRING ABOUT LIBERATION

Cone claims, "it may not be entirely clear why God elected Israel to be God's people, but one point is evident. The election is inseparable from the event of the exodus:

You have seen what I did to the Egyptians, and how I bore you on eagles' wings and brought you to myself. Now therefore, if you will obey my voice and keep my covenant, you shall be my own possession among all people… (Exodus 19:4-5a)."[11] It is clear to me that God is concerned about the liberation of His people. Liberation is achieved through His process. It is through this process that the people of God depend on God to take them from bondage to freedom. God always identifies with oppression. The oppressed become His people. According to Cone, "If the history of Israel and New Testament description of the historical Jesus reveals that God is a God who is identified with Israel because it is an oppressed community, the resurrection of Jesus means that all oppressed people become His people."[12] The oppressed are connected with a God who sees them in their oppressive conditions and delivers them from them all.

GOD LIBERATED ISRAEL FROM OPPRESSION

To be elected or chosen by God is a central theme for the children of Israel. Like the children of Israel, the church has been chosen to do the work of liberation. Owen

---
[11] Cone, 2.
[12] Ibid., 3.

Thomas argues that, "the fundamental theme of these doctrines is the conviction of the biblical authors that God has chosen Israel to be God's own people and to be the agent or instrument in the fulfillment of the divine purposes for humanity."[13] God elected the children of Israel to bring about a plan in which the Messiah would ultimately come. Although they were elected by God, it is a common practice of God to select groups and individuals to bring about His perfect plan in the world. Edward Smith, in *the Doctrine of Providence & Revelation: an Introduction to Philosophy and Theology,* points out that John Calvin claimed that:

> Israel was the first elect, and divine elect also encompassed the Gentiles. A remnant remains in every group that God has chosen depicting God's righteousness. However, Calvin wanted to move away from the group concept and closes here stressing the significance that God chooses 'individuals.' Divine Election then, becomes a personal and individual concern. Salvation involves an individual relationship with God through Jesus Christ."[14]

In the believer's relationship with God, they discover that perfect and divine purpose that God has in store for the believer. Church leaders who lead others must have a

---

[13] Thomas and Wondra, 211.
[14] Edward L. Smith, *the Doctrine of Providence & Revelation: an Introduction to Philosophy and Theology* (Riverdale, Ga.: The Research Center Press, 2001), 47.

relationship with God so they can reach others for the glory of God.

GOD APPOINTED MOSES

Moses discovers in his conversation with God that in spite of his insufficiency God was going to deliver His people. I contend that like Moses, we all have insufficiencies but we realize that leadership should not be avoided. God informs Moses that God was going to liberate because God saw their oppression. This is the very nature of a liberating God who sees the hardships and persecutions of a people. God is always moving His people to a place of liberation and freedom. Bondi asserts, "Leadership has to do with the movement of people through time and change."[15] Although Moses felt insufficient, God still used him to bring about liberation. Exodus chapter three gives this account of the liberating attributes of God and the choosing of a leader who feels insufficient:

> "[7] The LORD said, "I have indeed seen the misery of my people in Egypt. I have heard them crying out because of their slave drivers, and I am concerned about their suffering. [8] So I have come down to rescue them from the hand of the Egyptians and to bring them up out of

---

[15] Thomas, 18.

that land into a good and spacious land, a land flowing with milk and honey—the home of the Canaanites, Hittites, Amorites, Perizzites, Hivites and Jebusites. ⁹ And now the cry of the Israelites has reached me, and I have seen the way the Egyptians are oppressing them. ¹⁰ So now, go. I am sending you to Pharaoh to bring my people the Israelites out of Egypt." ¹¹ But Moses said to God, "Who am I, that I should go to Pharaoh and bring the Israelites out of Egypt?" ¹² And God said, "I will be with you. And this will be the sign to you that it is I who have sent you: When you have brought the people out of Egypt, you^a will worship God on this mountain."¹³ Moses said to God, "Suppose I go to the Israelites and say to them, 'The God of your fathers has sent me to you,' and they ask me, 'What is his name?' Then what shall I tell them?" ¹⁴ God said to Moses, "I AM WHO I AM.^{b} This is what you are to say to the Israelites: 'I AM has sent me to you.'" ¹⁵ God also said to Moses, "Say to the Israelites, 'The LORD,^{c} the God of your fathers—the God of Abraham, the God of Isaac and the God of Jacob—has sent me to you.' This is my name forever, the name by which I am to be remembered from generation to generation."¹⁶

---

^{a} The Hebrew is plural.
^{b} Or *I WILL BE WHAT I WILL BE*
^{c} The Hebrew for *LORD* sounds like and may be derived from the Hebrew for *I AM* in verse 14.
¹⁶Exodus 3:7-15

GOD SAW THE OPPRESSION AND SENT MOSES

God saw the oppression of his people and sent Moses to liberate them from the oppressor. It appears that Moses felt insufficient but God still chose him to be their leader. Cone points out "by delivering this people from Egyptian bondage and inaugurating the covenant on the basis of that historical event, God is revealing as the God of the oppressed, involved in their history, liberating them from human bondage."[17] It is interesting to note that theologians view God from many different angles and perspectives as it relates to liberation. Owen C. Thomas points out that, "womanist theology focuses on the biblical picture of Jesus rather than philosophical and theological discussion of the person of Christ. Jesus' ministry with the poor, the outcast, and the oppressed reveals the true character of God: 'God is as Jesus does.' Further, Jesus' death and resurrection manifests God's ability and willingness to 'make a way out of no way,' overcoming the seeming hopelessness of the oppressed." [18] It appears that European theologians view God from a philosophical and theological understanding without looking into the lens of

---

[17] Cone, 2.
[18] Thomas and Wondra, 175.

the oppressed. If theology is going to be relevant, is must speak to the ills in all communities.

GOD IS AT GOD'S BEST LIBERATING THOSE WHO ARE OPPRESSED

It appears to me that God is at God's best liberating those who are oppressed by the hand of the oppressor. Leonardo Boff, *in The Modern Theologians,* claims, "liberation theology adopts 'the Exodus as a paradigm of all liberation,' with liberation from (the oppression of Pharaoh) and liberation to (entry into the Promised Land). But the agency of liberation has now been given to a new Israel: 'God is no longer the old God of the Torah,' but 'a God of infinite goodness...He draws near in grace, going far beyond anything prescribed or ordained by the law.' "[19] As God liberates Gods people, God is not confined to a set of rules, regulations, or hidden agendas. When church leaders realize the awesomeness of God's power, they can be assured that God has the power to work the impossible. This needs to be reinforced because of their need to exercise more faith. I contend that God is genuinely

---

[19] David Ford, *The Modern Theologians: An Introduction to Christian Theology in the Twentieth Century* (Malden, Massachusetts: Blackwell Publishers Inc., 1997), 616.

concerned about the oppression of God's people. Cone claims that:

> Later stages of Israelite history also show that God is particularly concerned about the oppressed within the community of Israel. The rise of Old Testament prophecy is due primarily to the lack of justice within that community. The prophets of Israel are prophets of social justice, reminding the people that Yahweh is the author of justice. It is important to note in this connection that the righteousness of God is not an abstract quality in the being of God, as with Greek philosophy.[20]

It is interesting to point out that whenever there is injustice in a society, God always raises up a prophet. The prophet Job is to speak on behalf of the oppressed and for God. The prophet speaks about how God is concerned about oppression and the disenfranchised.

GOD IS ADVOCATING FOR THE POOR AND LESS FORTUNATE

In the history of God's revealed word, the Bible indicates how very active God is advocating for the poor and less fortunate because of His love for them. According to Cone, "it is rather God's active involvement in history, making right what human beings have made wrong. The

---

[20] Cone, 2.

consistent theme in Israelite prophecy is Yahweh's concern for the lack of social, economic, and political justice for those who are poor and unwanted in society. Yahweh, according to Hebrew prophecy, will not tolerate injustice against the poor; God will vindicate the poor."[21] The poor have a divine helper who steps into their situation and brings about an awesome transformation from oppression and conformation of His great love. It is the very nature of God to set at liberty those who were marginalized and oppressed. J. Deotis Roberts argued that the theme of love is just as important as His freedom. This love according to Roberts, "heals the brokenness between [people], it overcomes estrangement, and it brings people together—it reconciles. Love is compassion. Love is redemptive… God is love; love is God."[22] I contend it is the task of leadership to push and promote the love of God to the marginalized and oppressed people because it is at the very heart of God's nature to liberate those marginalized and oppressed.

God is using a process to bring about liberation to the oppressed. He has elected Israel to be His people in whom he would liberate from oppression. He appointed a leader by the name of Moses, even thou Moses felt

---

[21] Ibid.
[22] James H. Evans, Jr., *We Have Been Believers* (Minneapolis: Fortress Press., 1992), 70.

insufficient to be their leader. In the midst of liberating His people, God is at His best liberating those who are oppressed by the hand of the oppressor and advocating for the poor and less fortunate because of His love for them. These are Gods mighty acts of liberation.

JESUS AS A LIBERATOR

The overall theme of the New Testament is liberation. It is my belief that the New Testament affirms that Jesus was a liberator. As previously stated, Jesus started his preaching ministry with these words: "The Spirit of the Lord is upon me, because he has anointed me to preach good news to the poor. He has sent me to proclaim release to the captives and the recovering of sight to the blind, to set at liberty those who are oppressed, to proclaim the acceptable year of the Lord [Luke 4:18-19]." This is a direct response to the oppression and suffering of God's people. Jesus has an agenda to liberate the people of God from their oppressor. Six liberating facts about Jesus as a liberator will be explored. The six liberating facts include:

(1) He started the ministry dealing with the forces that had God's people in oppression.

(2) His public ministry focused on those who were marginalized and considered the outcast.

(3) His messages and life was about liberation and justice for all.

(4) His religion is a clear response to the oppression and suffering of His people.

(5) He had many followers but He equipped the twelve to turn the world upside down to institute change in a world that resisted change.

(6) He taught and equipped the twelve concerning liberation.

JESUS' MINISTRY DEALT WITH PEOPLE IN OPPRESSION

Jesus started the ministry dealing with the forces that had God's people in oppression. Jesus enters conflict with Satan and the power of the world; He is at war to liberate Gods people from bondage. Cone has suggested that, "the conflict with Satan and the powers of this world, the condemnation of the rich, the insistence that the kingdom of God is for the poor, and the locating of his ministry among the poor—these and other features of the career of Jesus show that his work was directed to the oppressed for the purpose of their liberation. To suggest that he was speaking of a 'spiritual' liberation fails to take seriously Jesus' thoroughly Hebrew view of human nature. Entering into the kingdom of God means that Jesus himself becomes the ultimate loyalty of humankind, for he is the kingdom."[23]

The gospel of Luke deals with the poor and the disfranchised as well. Warren W. Wiersbe points out "In this Gospel you meet individuals as well as crowds, women and children as well as men, poor people as well as rich people, and sinners along with saints. It's a book with a message for *everybody*, because Luke's emphasis is on the universality of Jesus Christ and His salvation: "good tidings of great joy, which shall be to all people (Luke 2:10)."[24] Jesus is liberating Gods people. Human beings are liberated to fight against the forces of the world. The very fact that Jesus arose from the grave means that God's liberating work is not only for the house of Israel but also for all who are enslaved by principalities and power of this world. David L. Smith argues that Jesus Christ was a liberator who is seen as Savior, Redeemer, and Power. He points out that, "Closely tied is the concept of Christ as Liberator.

---

[23] Cone, 3.

[24] Warren W. Wiersbe, *The Bible Exposition Commentary*, "An Exposition of the New Testament Comprising the Entire 'BE' Series"-- Jkt. (Wheaton, Ill.: Victor Books, 1996, c1989), Mk 16:19.

'Liberation must be understood in its totality as removal of all that which keeps the African in bondage, all that makes him less than God intended him to be.' The idea is that Jesus has the power to liberate from fear, illness, and evil, as well as from oppression, racism, and exploitation. That Jesus identified in His own earthly life with the poor, needy, and defenseless endears Him all the more to black Africans."[25] I assert that the total leadership has to focus on these ills by becoming more responsible in their quest to be like Him. It is through the equipping of leaders that the church can deal with these ills. Leadership must have a kingdom agenda that liberates the mind, body and soul.

JESUS FOCUSED ON THE MARGINALIZED AND THE OUTCAST

The public ministry of Jesus focused on those who were marginalized and considered the outcast.

Owens C. Thomas claims that:

Jesus proclamation of the reign of God is enacted in healing the sick, who are also marginalized and impoverished by their illnesses, in casting out demons, and in befriending prostitutes and sinners, viewed as outcasts

---

[25] David L. Smith, *A Handbook of Contemporary Theology* (Grand Rapids: Baker Books, 1992), 217.

by the religious establishment. Jesus ministry proclaims and shows the God of life, and his suffering and death are acts of the powers of death in response to the life he has lived and the message he has proclaimed; God's resurrection of Jesus vindicates both Jesus' life and God's will for life abundant in opposition to the forces of death.[26]

The followers of Jesus continued to focus on the ministry for the downcast and the oppressed. The followers knew that if they received the downcast and the oppressed, they received the Lord and His blessing. Jesus said in the gospel of Matthew, "I tell you the truth, anything you refused to do for even the least of my people here, you refused to do for me."[27] Thomas claims "special concern for the marginalized continues in the earliest church's focus on ministry to the poor, widows, and outcasts, and in the decision to hold possessions in common (Act4:32-35). Paul criticizes the church in Corinth for allowing socioeconomic status to disrupt the church as it gathers for the Eucharist and fellowship (I Cor. 11:21-22). The church's mission includes continuing Jesus' own ministry of proclamation of good news to the poor and the captive."[28] I believe that the leadership of the church should allow the same mandate

---

[26] Thomas and Wondra, 192.

[27] *The Everyday Bible : New Century Version* (Nashville, TN.: Thomas Nelson, Inc., 2005), Mt 25:45.

[28] Ibid, 194.

that Jesus proclaims to be the same mandate by which they do ministry. The mandate was to preach the good news to the poor and set at liberty those who are oppressed. It is imperative for church leaders to keep the mission and ministry for the least of these. In the words of Martin Luther King, Jr. and Howard Thurman, "oppression contravenes every aspect of this 'beloved community.'"[29] Jesus spent his time and ministry preaching to this beloved community. This infested community was full of injustices, moral decay, and social unrest. It is the responsibility of the church and its leaders to address injustices, moral decay and social unrest by having programs and ministries that will combat these needs.

JESUS MESSAGES WERE ABOUT LIBERATION AND JUSTICE FOR ALL

Jesus messages to people in general and his life style were about liberation and justice for all. James Evans points out that Howard Thurman in his book *Jesus and the Disinherited* takes a serious look at, "what is the significance of the religion of Jesus for 'people with their backs against the wall.' Second, why is it that Christianity

---

[29] Ibid.

is impotent in dealing effectively 'with the issues of discrimination and injustice on the basis of race, religion, and national origin.' For Thurman, it is not a question of the moral obligation that Christianity lays upon those what have much, but the existential meaning of Christianity for those who have little or nothing."[30] The crucial question according to Thurman related to, "who is Jesus for the downtrodden."[31] According to Evans, Thurman identifies three central features of Jesus in the biblical narratives. These three central features are paramount to the overall theme of Jesus being a liberator. First, Jesus was a Jew. Since he was a Jew, he had a specific ethnic, racial, and religious identity. Thurman believes, "it is impossible for Jesus to be understood outside of the sense of community which Israel held with God…The Christian Church has tended to overlook its Judaic origins, but the fact is that Jesus of Nazareth was a Jew of Palestine when he went about this Father's business, announcing the acceptable year of the Lord."[32] Second, Jesus was a poor Jew. Since he was a poor Jew, according to Evans, "his condition of material want cemented his solidarity with the poor of his time. Further, his poverty takes on added significance in the

---

[30] Evans, 83.
[31] Ibid.
[32] Ibid., 84.

light of his designation as the human one, or the Son of Man."[33] I believe this is significant because as a liberator he can relate to those in whom he is liberating. He is not a liberator who is in a far and distant land. It is important that the church keep in mind that we are agents of light in the midst of darkness. They cannot be aloft to human degradation.

Thurman points out, "the economic predicament with which he was identified in birth placed him initially with the great mass of men on earth. The masses of the people are poor. If we dare take the position that in Jesus there was at work some radical destiny, it would be safe to say that in his poverty he was more truly Son of man than he would have been if the incident of family or birth had made him a rich son of Israel."[34] Third, Jesus was a member of an oppressed minority. He shared the oppression that comes with the community. The Roman Empire oppressed the Jews of Palestine in their social and political context. Jesus grew up in this particular context. Thurman points out, "it is utterly fantastic to assume that Jesus grew to manhood untouched by the surging currents of the common life that made up the climate of Palestine.

---

[33] Ibid.
[34] Ibid.

Not only must he have been aware of them; that he was affected by them is a most natural observation."[35] These experiences help shape the religion of Jesus. They will also help shape the values of the church as well.

THE RELIGION OF JESUS IS A RESPONSE TO OPPRESSION AND SUFFERING

The religion of Jesus is a clear response to the oppression and suffering of his people. Thurman argues that Jesus had two options in the Israelite culture in relation to Rome. He points out that the "first option was nonresistance, in which the oppressed Jews could either imitate the dominant group or assimilate their culture and traditions, or simply withdraw, as far as possible, from the oppressive group and be content with occasional displays of contempt. The second option was resistance, which manifests itself most often in armed struggle. This type of resistance has its appeal among the oppressed, but that appeal is often tragic in the sense that it must destroy part of what it seeks to preserve."[36] Thurman believes that the religion of Jesus is a different form of resistance; a

---
[35] Ibid.
[36] Ibid.

resistance that is summed up in the statement that Jesus made the kingdom of God is in us. Evans states that, "this internal, or spiritual, liberation is not sought at the expense of social and political freedom. In fact, Thurman states that an otherworldly focus in religion is the Achilles' heel of traditional Christianity. 'The desperate opposition to Christianity rests in the fact that it seems, in the last analysis, to be a betrayal of the Negro into the hands of his enemies by focusing his attention upon heaven, forgiveness, love and the like.'"[37] It appears to me that the religion of Jesus is a clear response to the oppression and suffering of his people. It is through suffering that Jesus understood the despair and dilemmas of his people. Leadership must understand that suffering is a part of the journey. As leaders, there must be an anticipation of some suffering along the way. Thurman makes an important argument that Jesus is a direct response to the uproar and injustices of the oppressed. He claims that:

> It seems clear that Jesus understood the anatomy of the relationship between his people and the Romans, and he interpreted the relationship against the background of the profoundest ethical insight of his own religious faith as he had found it in the heart of the prophets of Israel. The solution which Jesus found for himself and for Israel, as they faced

---

[37] Ibid.

the hostility of the Greco-Roman world, becomes the word and the work of redemption for all the cast down people in the every generation and in every age. I mean this quite literally. I do not ignore the theological and metaphysical interpretation of the Christian doctrine of salvation. But the underprivileged everywhere have long since abandoned any hope that this type of salvation deals with the crucial issues by which their days are turned into despair without consolation. The basic fact is that Christianity as it was born in the mind of this Jewish thinker appears as a technique of survival for the oppressed. That it became, through the intervening years, a religion of the powerful and dominant, used sometimes as an instrument of oppression, must not tempt us into believing that it was thus in the mind and life of Jesus.[38]

I contend that whenever there is an injustice concerning a group of people, the whole nation suffers because of it. The nation of Israel is an excellent example. Thomas points out that "Inequitable distribution of power and resources, the perpetuation of social arrangements through violence and coercion, and the devaluing of human life warps and diminishes everyone who is caught up in it, hinders and breaks right relations among people, and violates God's creation and providence. In others words, oppression is a form of sin, producing long-range and large-scale

---

[38] Ibid., 85.

alienation from God and from others. It is sin whose consequences are borne by others through social, economic, and cultural means that often seem intractable."[39] As a liberator, Jesus dealt with the sins of humankind. He led them from their oppressor by showing them a better way. Leadership in the church must model for those around them a better way of living by dealing with those who are oppressed by sin.

JESUS EQUIPPED THE TWELVE DISCIPLES

Jesus had many followers but he equipped the twelve disciples to turn the world upside down to institute change in a world that resisted change. Jesus taught followers about denying self and following him but the followers refused at times to follow Jesus. The twelve disciples were committed to following Jesus even though the crowd refused. The disciples validated that committed followers in spite of insufficiency can make a difference. On one occasion when the crowd walked away from Him, Jesus asked the disciples, "Will you also go away? Will the tides of popular opinion of the world make you go under? Simon Peter answered him, 'Lord, to whom shall we go?

---

[39] Thomas and Wondra, 195.

You have the words of eternal life." [40] The twelve disciples were committed to following Jesus because He had the words of eternal life. The answer of Simon Peter, according to Johnson, "contains a great assumption, namely, that man must have someone to whom he may go. The souls of men are hungry, crushed, baffled, and perplexed, and cry out not for something but for someone. Men cannot live without a master, without a guide, without a revealer, a liberator, and a reconciler. Man is so constituted that he cannot live alone, cannot grope his own way except searching for the one who shall be his rest."[41] The words of Augustine says, "Thou hast made us for thyself, O God, and our hearts are restless until they find that rest which is in Thee."[42] It is in God that leaders find their perfect peace and rest. The twelve disciples discovered that Jesus offered a reassuring peace and rest that the world could not give. The leadership in the church must rely on the sovereign hand of God to grant them the peace that they need for the journey to be great leaders.

---

[40] Johnson, 270.
[41] Ibid., 271.
[42] Ibid.

JESUS EQUIPPED THE TWELVE CONCERNING LIBERATIONS

Jesus taught and equipped the twelve concerning liberations. He sent them on missions of liberation throughout Israel.

Leon Morris, in *New Testament Theology,* has suggested concerning the mission that:

> Jesus specifically told his disciples not to go to the Gentiles or even to the Samaritans (Act 10:5); this mission was to 'the lost sheep of the house of Israel' (v.6). Some features of his charge seem to apply only to that mission, whereas others are of wider application. Be that as it may, on this occasion Jesus gave the disciples authority over demons and disease (10:1, 8). He sent them without material resources; God would look after them. The burden of their message was 'the kingdom of heaven has drawn near' (10:7). They went thus with the message of peace, and Jesus gave directions as to what their reactions should be when they were received peacefully and when they were not (10:11-15)."[43]

It appears that their mission of liberation was to the oppressed and marginalized. Jesus led the disciples to do greater work then He would do. The disciples fulfilled the mission in spite of the many obstacles that were before

---

[43] Leon Morris, *New Testament Theology* (Grand Rapids: Zondervan, 1986), 140.

them. The leadership in the church must keep the mission before them in order to do a greater work for Christ. The mission gives leadership focus and clarity. Cornel West asserts that, "Quality leadership is neither the product of one great individual nor the results of odd historical accidents. Rather, it comes from deeply bred traditions and communities that shape and mold talented and gifted persons. Without a vibrant tradition of resistance passed on to new generations, there can be no nurturing of a collective and critical consciousness-only professional conscientiousness survives."[44]

In conclusion, Jesus demonstrated a perfect model for liberation. Jesus started the ministry dealing with the forces that had God's people in oppression. His public ministries focused on those who were marginalized and who were considered the outcast. Jesus' whole message and life were about liberation and justice for all. It is apparent that the religion of Jesus is a clear response to the oppression and suffering of his people. Jesus had many followers but he taught and equipped the twelve to turn the world upside down to institute change in a world the resisted change and brought about liberation to those who

---

[44] Cornel West, *Race Matters* (New York: Vintage Books, 2001), 56.

were marginalized. Jesus is a positive and effective leader for the church to follow and model after because He is a leader among leaders.

HUMAN LIBERATION

The Bible paints a picture of humanity being delivered from the hands of the oppressor. From the Exodus event to Jesus proclaiming the messages of liberation, it is about God liberating His people. God is at the forefront leading men and women to bring about liberation for His people. He uses whom He desires to bring about this process. In spite of their conditions and character, God chooses imperfect people to bring about His perfect plan. I will examine human liberation from three perspectives. The three perspectives are:

(1) It is vital that one look at the Bible for motifs that will help aid in understanding the Bible and human liberation.
(2) Leaders should consider the biblical hermeneutic concerning human liberation.
(3) Human liberation in not for people of color only but persons who find themselves oppressed by a culture of oppressors.

BIBLE MOTIFS THAT WILL AID IN UNDERSTANDING

It is vital that one look at the Bible for motifs that will help aid in understanding the Bible and human liberation. Latta R. Thomas in *Biblical Faith and the Black American* has suggested that the Bible is concerned for people from all occupations especially those who are oppressed and need liberation. According to J. Deotis Roberts, Thomas has set forth four biblical interpretations for evangelical and liberation motifs that will help aid in understanding the Bible and human liberation.

> First, the Bible is a collective document that grew out of and is about God's liberation of people from human sin and oppression. Second, the Bible pictures the real God of heaven and earth and of Jesus Christ as always concentrating his liberating efforts and concerns where human beings are in need. Third, before the Bible can be seen in all its liberating purity and power, effort must be made to identify and cut through those motives, myths, and interpretations, whether deliberate or accidental, which result in the attempts to twist the Bible in support of Black enslavement and White racism. Fourth, black people need the liberating power and direction available in the biblical faith as never before, and should fully embrace them.[45]

---

[45] Roberts, 48.

Thomas sees the Bible as a means for the liberation of the oppressed people. The leaders in the church must have a deep appreciation of the Bible and its connection with liberation. The Bible is the final authority in the church. Therefore, leaders must know the word of God. Thomas sees the Bible as an important document to help liberate and inform those who are oppressed. Thomas understands the Bible to be a book of physical and spiritual liberation. His argument is that, "In reality the Bible, when allowed to come through without human tampering by people with shallow minds and evil motives, not only *does not* support human oppression, but also *urges human rebellion* against mistreatment of human beings as a matter of commitment to the God of heaven, earth and history. The central theme of the New Testament is that God himself came to man's hopeless and helpless situation (incarnation) to lift human being from the condition characterized by human sin and misery, and through Jesus, the Christ, began his work with the farthest down- the have-nots, the enslaved, the outcasts, the wounded, and the 'nobodies' of this world."[46] I assert that when leaders in the church connect with the God of the Bible, they can truly

---

[46] Ibid., 46.

liberate others from their oppression. There must be a connection with God in order for liberation to take place.

BIBLICAL HERMENEUTICS CONCERNING LIBERATION

In looking for human liberation, leaders should consider the biblical hermeneutics concerning liberation. Roberts points out that Thomas is similar to Cone. Thomas calls witness to the Moses of the Exodus and the author of Luke in support of his outlook on biblical interpretation. It is evident that Roberts, Thomas, and Cone adhere to similar biblical hermeneutics concerning human liberation. Roberts's stated, "Elsewhere I have discussed how the West African understanding of God was similar to the biblical God, especially regarding divine creation and providence. Black slaves brought from Africa to America a view of community that emphasized individual responsibility within community, the relation between human beings, and the relation between the living and the dead. Religion embraced all of life."[47] I contend it is our religious experiences that we understand God and His plan for liberation in our lives. It is in these experiences that

---

[47] Ibid., 47.

church leaders are able to understand what people are going through and help them through the liberation process. Cone argues, "persuasively that there can be no true reconciliation between oppressed people and their oppressors without liberation of the oppressed. All talk about reconciliation without liberation only blesses injustice. But it is also true that there is no true liberation without reconciliation. True liberation means liberation also from the hostility and alienation that destroy the humanity of both oppressed people and their oppressors."[48] I assert that when reconciliation takes place in the church, it opens the avenue for liberation for all. It is difficult for liberation to occur for everyone when it is targeted for one group. Leaders must assert liberation for everyone, those that have and those that have not.

HUMAN LIBERATION IS NOT JUST FOR PEOPLE OF COLOR

Human liberation is not just for people of color only but persons who find themselves oppressed by a culture of oppressors. Womanist theologians, Jacquelyn Grant and

---

[48] Shirley C. Guthrie, *Christian Doctrine: Revised Edition* (Louisville: Westminster/John Knox Press.1994), 407.

Delores Williams, stated that, "there is a 'liberating word' in the Bible, although at the same time they believe that the use of the Bible must be carefully constructed, since, in addition to serving liberation, the Bible has historically served as a tool of oppression against women and ethnic and sexual minorities."[49] Although there has been many strives in hermeneutics, the womanist theologians believe that there is still a touch of sexism by black male theologians in their interpretation. Womanist theologians claimed that, "although black male theologians have readily identified the ways in which Euro-Americans have appropriated the Bible to suit their purposes in showing themselves to be racially and morally superior to blacks, these same male theologians have taken advantage of the way in which traditional Western theology promotes a belief in the inferiority of women. Despite the difficulties involved in appropriating the Bible for liberal causes, womanists agree with other Christian feminists that the Bible cannot simply be jettisoned by liberationists, because it has been and continues to form the foundation of daily faith and life of many Christian women."[50] Therefore, if liberation theology is going to be wholesome for the

---

[49] Donald W. Musser & Joseph L. Price, *A New Handbook of Christian Theologians* (Nashville: Abingdon Press. 1996),515.
[50] Ibid.

oppressed, it must address every arena of oppression. I believe that the leadership in the church must look at avenues to bring about liberation to all people, regardless of sex, race, or class. There are still persons in society that believe that God only uses certain people and genders. The church must be liberated from that by sound doctrine.

In addition to the womanist theologians feeling that there is still oppression brought on by their counter parts, Latin Americans have their concerns with oppression as well. It is important to note that the whole process of liberation theology came from Latin America. The movement was set in place for the poor of Latin America that they might assert their human dignity and their status as daughters and sons of God. Gustavo Gutierrez asserts that" the breakthrough or irruption- as it has been called- of the poor in Latin America not only left its mark on the beginning of the theology of liberation but is daily becoming more urgent and massive, even where the effort is made to hide or repress it. This has simply reinforced the fact that the entrance of the poor onto center stage in Latin American society and the Latin American church has plowed new furrows for Christian life and reflection."[51] I

---

[51] Gustavo Gutierrez, *We Drink From Our Own Wells: The Spiritual Journey of A People*(Mary knoll, New York: Orbis Books, 1998), 1.

believe that liberation is attainable for everyone. The poor and the outcast should be on the radar of church leaders in this context because they are usually those who are left behind.

LIBERATION THEOLOGY IS A LOOK AT GOD WORKING

In conclusion, liberation theology is at look a God working through the life of His Son and others to bring about liberation to the outcast, the overlooked, and the oppressed. Over the last thirty years, James Evans and other theologians have moved black theology into a broader, multidimensional understanding of liberation. Evans has taken up the task of outlining the dimensions of liberation that are paramount in the fight against oppression. Although James Cone's sociopolitical liberation has added physical, spiritual, and cultural understanding of liberation, it must be seen as one piece. Evans asserts that, "physical liberation refers to the innate desire of all human beings to enjoy freedom of movement and association and the rights of self-determination. Spiritual empowerment is that dimension of the liberation struggle in which African Americans come to understand

and reclaim their intrinsic worth as human beings. Cultural liberation refers to freedom from negative self-images, symbols, and stereotypes."[52] It is through these dimensions that leaders see liberation at work. I assert that the leadership must grab hold to these dimensions to make a difference in the people that they serve. Cleophus J. LaRue is clear in pointing out that, "An overemphasis on any one of the three dimensions leads to an imbalance in the others. Consequently, Evans cautions against viewing the liberation motif as unidimensional. In its unidimensional extremes, it tends to be identified with sociopolitical justice at one end or a mere inward spiritual piety at the other."[53] In order for true liberation to exist, it must exist for all people regardless of race, sex, or creed. There must be a balance in the entire dimension. In essence, human liberation is about a vital look at the Bible for motifs that will help aid in understanding the Bible and human liberation, leaders must consider the biblical hermeneutic concerning human liberation and it is not for people of color only but persons who find themselves oppressed by a culture of oppressors.

---

[52] Cleophus J. LaRue, *The Heart of Black Preaching* (Louisville: Westminster John Knox Press, 2000), 118.
[53] Ibid., 119.

CHAPTER 2 - GOD, THE "HOLY" LIBERATOR

Fill in the blank

1. A theology of _____ must be the foundation of this God mandated experience because it will show us how God is liberating His people.

2. Church leaders must believe not only in the _____ and _____ aspects of church work but they must believe it is ordained by God.

3. Church leaders both _____ and _____ must have a level of theological training that is consistent with their leadership responsibility.

4. Leaders must keep in mind that _____ is at the center of Christian religion.

5. There can be no good _____ if it is not connected with the downcast and underprivileged.

6. God was about _____ those who are on the bottom of the social order.

7. Leaders must keep in mind that the _____ event was a part of God's liberation plan.

8. Leaders must realize that the exodus of the children of Israel is a _____ of a God who is the God of and for those who labor are heavy burdened.

9. It is through liberation that God uses leaders to deliver his people from the snares of being _____.

10. It is the responsibility of total leadership in the church to _____ and _____ those who are marginalized by society in giving them the helping hand that they need.

GOD AS A LIBERATOR

Answer True or False

1. ____ God used a process to liberate them.
2. ____ God elected Israel to be His people.

3. _____ God appointed a leader by the name of Samuel in spite of his insufficiencies.
4. _____ God is at His worst when liberating those who are oppressed by the hand of the oppressor.
5. _____ In the history of God's revealed Word, the Bible indicates how very active God is in advocating for the poor and less fortunate because of His love for them.
6. _____ God is not concerned about the liberation of His people.
7. _____ Liberation is achieved through His process.
8. _____ God always identifies with the oppressed.
9. _____ The oppressed are connected with a God who sees them in their oppressive condition and delivers them from them all.
10. _____ Moses felt sufficient to lead the children of Israel.
11. _____ If theology is going to be relevant, it must speak to the ills of community.
12. _____ Jesus started his ministry dealing with the forces that had God's people in oppression.
13. _____ His public ministry focused on those who were high class and the upper-class.

14. ____ His messages and life was about himself and nobody else.

15. ____ His religion is a clear response to the oppression and suffering of his people.

16. ____ He had many followers but he equipped the twelve to turn the world upside-down to institute change in a world that resisted change.

17. ____ He taught and equipped the twelve concerning liberation.

18. ____ Leaders should always consider the Biblical hermeneutic concerning liberation.

19. ____ It is vital that one look at the Bible for motifs that will help aid in understanding the Bible in human liberation.

20. ____ Human liberation is not for people of color only, but for persons who find themselves oppressed by a culture of oppressors.

CHAPTER III

THE "HOLY" CONNECTION IN THE OLD TESTAMENT

The contemporary church is comprised of all kinds of leaders. There are leaders who assume that they are leaders just because they hold the title of a leader. They have been given the title pastor, deacon, trustee, president, chairman, etc. The sad fact is that many are unaware of the position that has been given them. If the contemporary church is to be relevant, it must take a serious look at the leadership of the church.

Leadership in the local church is different from other sectors in our society. The church is not an organization but an organism that lives and gives birth to help hurting humanity. Geoffrey V. Guns in *Spiritual Leadership: A Guide to Developing Spiritual Leaders in the Church* suggested, "the church is a spiritual organism, called into being by God to achieve the purposes of God in the world. Therefore, those who lead are called by God to fulfill God's purpose and not their own agenda."[54] This

---

[54] Geoffrey V. Guns. *Spiritual Leadership: A Guide to Developing Spiritual Leaders in the Church* (Lithonia, GA.: Orman Press, Inc., 2000), 45.

book will look at leadership models from a biblical perspective from the Old and New Testament and how leaders dealt with the paradigm change.

OLD TESTAMENT MODEL

There were many great leaders who lead Israel toward their purpose and plan that God had for them. I contend that Moses was one of the most important and significant leaders in the life of Israel. By examining Moses, it is in no way demeaning the significance of the other great patriarchs. They were all called to do a certain task for the people of God during a particular season. Moses was an ideal model for leadership and effective in leading change, especially for those in bondage, in the Old Testament. Moses had leadership qualities and characteristics that made him an ideal leader in the Old Testament. These include:

(1) He was commissioned by God to lead God's people to a land flowing with milk and honey.
(2) He was courageous to confront the many challenges of dealing with Pharaoh although he felt insufficient.

(3) He was committed to God and offered hope in spite of the contention in the crowd.

(4) He was confident that God would establish his leadership.

This research will explore each of these aspects that made Moses a unique and ideal leader in the Old Testament.

MOSES WAS COMMISSIONED BY GOD

Moses was an ideal leader in the Old Testament because he was commissioned by God to lead God's people to a land flowing with milk and honey. Moses was the first to lead a congregation versus a single family in the Old Testament. He was to lead the children of Israel out of bondage after God heard their cry from oppression. Gutierrez points out that, "the Jewish people set out in quest of an encounter with God. But in a way this encounter was already a reality at the beginning of the journey. Even when the Israelites were still in Egypt, Yahweh expressed close and sympathetic awareness of their situation."[55] In chapter three of Exodus, the writer makes it clear that God is calling Moses to lead His people. It states,

---

[55] Gutierrez, 77

"Now Moses was tending the flock of Jethro his father-in-law, the priest of Midian, and he led the flock to the far side of the desert and came to Horeb, the mountain of God. ² There the angel of the LORD appeared to him in flames of fire from within a bush. Moses saw that though the bush was on fire it did not burn up. ³ So Moses thought, "I will go over and see this strange sight—why the bush does not burn up." ⁴ When the LORD saw that he had gone over to look, God called to him from within the bush, "Moses! Moses!" And Moses said, "Here I am." ⁵ "Do not come any closer," God said. "Take off your sandals, for the place where you are standing is holy ground." ⁶ Then he said, "I am the God of your father, the God of Abraham, the God of Isaac and the God of Jacob." At this, Moses hid his face, because he was afraid to look at God. ⁷ The LORD said, "I have indeed seen the misery of my people in Egypt. I have heard them crying out because of their slave drivers, and I am concerned about their suffering. ⁸ So I have come down to rescue them from the hand of the Egyptians and to bring them up out of that land into a good and spacious land, a land flowing with milk and honey—the home of the Canaanites, Hittites, Amorites, Perizzites, Hivites and Jebusites. ⁹ And now the cry of the Israelites has reached me, and I have seen the way the Egyptians are oppressing them. ¹⁰ So now, go. I am sending you to Pharaoh to bring my people the Israelites out of Egypt." [56]

---

[56] Exodus 3:1-10

Moses received his calling on the backside of the desert keeping Jethro's (his father-in-law) flock. Although Moses was highly educated and accustomed to the comfort of the palace, he was in a profession that was considered and held in low esteem. Herding sheep was not a highly sort after profession because it was for peasants. While herding the sheep, Moses had an encounter with the creator. It is vital that leaders have this encounter because of the obstacles that are before them. Moses turned to see, and then God spoke to him. Leroy Eims in *Be the Leader you were Meant to be: Biblical Principles of Leadership* has suggested that:

> [T]he first thing the Lord did was reveal Himself to Moses. Moses was certain that it was God who spoke to him (see vv.5-6). This is something that you must be sure about in your own mind. When someone comes to ask you to serve in one way or another, make certain that God is in it. Don't budge an inch in either direction- either yes or no- until you have determined the will of God in the matter.[57]

It is through these encounters that leaders have the assurances that God is going to give what they need for the journey. All leaders need an encounter with God for liberating those around them. If more leaders had an

---

[57] Leroy Eims, *Be the Leader you were Meant to be: Biblical Principles of Leadership* (Wheaton, Ill.: Victor Books, 1977), 9.

encounter with God, it would make leading more effective. At the commissioning of Moses, God instructs him to take off his shoes as a sign of reverence. James M. Freeman in *Manners & Customs of the Bible* has suggested that, "Orientals are as careful to remove their shoes or sandals before entering a house, or a place of worship, as we remove our hats. Piles of shoes, slippers, or sandals, may be seen at the doors of Mohammedan mosques and of Indian pagodas; it is a mark of respect due to those places. Moses was in this way directed to show his reverence for the Divine Presence."[58] Moses shows his reverence to God by taking off his shoes. In accepting the call to leadership, one must have a reverence to God and the people of God. The matter of leadership should be weighed very carefully by persons before they take on leadership responsibilities and be certain that it is the will of God that you take on the responsibility. Eims points out that, "since God is concerned with what we do, He will make His will known. He promises to do so. 'I will instruct thee and teach thee in the way which thou shalt go: I will guide thee with Mine eye' (Ps. 32:8)."[59]

---

[58] James M. Freeman, *Manners & Customs of the Bible* (New Kensington, Pa.: Whitaker House, 1996), 61.
[59] Eims, 9.

MOSES WAS COURAGEOUS TO CONFRONT THE CHALLENGES

Moses was an ideal leader in the Old Testament because he was courageous to confront the challenges of dealing with Pharaoh although Moses felt insufficient. On the one hand Pharaoh, according to J. David Pleins, "would not give up without a fight. Pharaoh's actions as both a product of ignorance and fear, ignorance of the good the Joseph had done (Exodus 1:8) and fear that the Israelites, being so numerous, will join in a coalition against Egypt that would supply a formidable opposition to the empire's hold on the region and the people therein (Exodus 1:9-10)."[60] The people of Israel were under a major taskmaster who was concerned about keeping them in bondage. In the midst of Israel being in bondage, God was calling Moses to be their liberator. When God presented to Moses the challenges concerning His people, Moses did not feel qualified for the task that God had given him and cried with the question, "Who am I." The question was so irrelevant that God did not address it. Eims points out, "therein lies one of the great secrets of leadership in the Christian

---

[60] J. David Pleins, *The Social Visions of the Hebrew Bible* (Louisville, Kentucky: Westminster John Knox Press, 2001), 159.

enterprise. God said, 'Certainly I will be with thee.' What the Lord was trying to get across to Moses was a powerful truth. He as much as said, 'Moses, it doesn't really matter who you are-whether you feel qualified or unqualified, whether you feel up to the task or not. The point is that I am going to be there. The statement I made to you still hold: I am come down to deliver them. I am going to do it, and I am going to give you the privilege of being in it with Me. You are My instrument of Deliverance."[61] Although Moses didn't feel sufficient, God still picked him to lead his people. Guns point out, "Moses did not feel that he was born with the special gifts or recognizable talents. In fact when called to go to Egypt to tell Pharaoh to release Israel from bondage, he pointed out his speaking handicaps. Then Moses said to the Lord, 'Please, Lord, I have never been eloquent, neither recently, nor in time past, nor since Thou hast spoken to Thy servant; for I am slow of speech and slow of tongue.' He lacked self-confidence."[62] I contend that God is not looking for leaders who feel that they have it all together or are sufficient, but leaders who look to Him for guidance and direction. Moses yields to the call of God in spite of his insufficiency. He was courageous in

---

[61] Ibid.,10.

[62] Guns, 54.

confronting Pharaoh and telling him to let God's people go. Pharaoh could have had him killed or imprisoned. Pharaoh was a brute and stubborn king. Michael Coogan in *The Oxford History of the Biblical World* has suggested that:

> Moses reluctantly accepting his commission, Moses goes back to Egypt, and initiates a series of patterned confrontations with Pharaoh. In each, Moses pleads with Pharaoh to 'let my people go,' Pharaoh is obdurate, Moses dramatically performs a miracle that devastates the Egyptians, Pharaoh first relents and then recants. In this way, nine spectacular plagues descend on the Egyptians: bloody water, frogs, gnats, flies, pestilence, boils, hail, locusts, and darkness. The series culminates with the tenth and deadliest plague, in which all firstborn Egyptians, human and animal, die; this both leads into and explains the origin of the Passover ritual. At long last Pharaoh permits the Israelites to leave, only to change his mind one last time and send his army after Moses. But his Egyptian soldiers meet their death in the Red (Reed) Sea, whose waters miraculously part for the fleeing Israelites and then close over Pharaoh's doomed army.[63]

I contend that Moses was so courageous because he saw what God did in Egypt while he was before Pharaoh. God showed Moses and the children of Israel that God was going to be with them. It was a time of insurmountable direction and guidance for the children of Israel. Every

---

[63] Michael D. Coogan ed., *The Oxford History of the Biblical World* (New York, NY: Oxford University Press, 1998), 59.

courageous leader must believe that God is going to do something outstanding in their lives. I assert that God can do greater works in the church if leaders would believe in the power of God to move obstacles. Warren Wiersbe in *Expository Outlines on the Old Testament* points out that:

> The plagues were actually a "declaration of war" against the gods of Egypt (see 12:12). The Nile River was worshiped as a god since it was their source of life (Deut. 11:10–12), and when Moses turned it into blood, God showed His power over the river. The goddess Heqt was pictured as a frog, the Egyptian symbol of resurrection. The plague of frogs certainly turned the people against Heqt! The lice and flies brought defilement to the people—a terrible blow, for Egyptians could not worship their gods unless they were the "cow-goddess" and Apis was the sacred bull. The gods and goddesses that controlled health and safety were attacked in the plagues of boils, hail, and locusts. The plague of darkness was the most serious, since Egypt worshiped the sun god, Ra, the chief of the gods. When the sun was blotted out for three days, it meant that Jehovah had conquered Ra. The final plague (the death of the firstborn) conquered Meskhemit the goddess of birth, and Hathor, her companion, both of whom were supposed to watch over the firstborn. All of these plagues made it clear that Jehovah was the true God![64]

---

[64]Warren W. Wiersbe, *Wiersbe's Expository Outlines on the Old Testament* (Wheaton, IL: Victor Books, 1993), Ex 5:1.

God showed His enemies and His people that Israel God was supreme to the gods of Egypt. If leaders are going to be successful, they have to follow the direction that God has outlined for them to follow. They were victories because God gave them a leader who listened to the voice and followed the direction given by God. Moses was a courageous leader because he confronted the many challenges that were before him.

MOSES WAS COMMITTED TO GOD

Moses was an ideal leader in the Old Testament because he was committed to God and offered hope in spite of the contention in the crowd. The first obstacle that Moses and the children of Israel had to contend with was being struck between a rock and a hard place. Terry Thomas claims that, "Their enclosed situation appeared to have been insurmountable. Through that incident, Jonathan Kirsch claims that 'Moses witnessed for the first time a characteristic of the Israelites that he would come to know with heartbreaking and sometimes maddening intimacy."[65]

---

[65] Terry Thomas. *An Exploration into the Task of Leadership*, lecture notes from cluster group/ Handout. 43.

In Exodus 14: 10-12 depicts the emotion and contention that the children of Israel had in their hearts. It reads:

> [10] As Pharaoh approached, the Israelites looked up, and there were the Egyptians, marching after them. They were terrified and cried out to the LORD. [11] They said to Moses, "Was it because there were no graves in Egypt that you brought us to the desert to die? What have you done to us by bringing us out of Egypt? [12] Didn't we say to you in Egypt, 'Leave us alone; let us serve the Egyptians'? It would have been better for us to serve the Egyptians than to die in the desert!"[66]

The children of Israel became hopeless because they saw Pharaoh and his army approaching and fear filled the camp. They were trapped at the Red (Reed) Sea with nowhere to turn. Contention and unbelief filled the camp and the people turned on their leader. John F. Walvoord in the *Bible Knowledge Commentary: an Exposition of the Scriptures* makes an interesting claim that:

> The reaction of the Israelites here was much the same throughout the book (cf. 5:21) in times of duress and fright. Though they cried out to the LORD, they had no confidence He could help. Quickly forgetting the past, they bitterly accused Moses of deceiving them by leading them into the desert to die. . . . Didn't we say . . . in Egypt, Leave

---

[66] Exodus 14:10-12.
cf. *confer*, compare

us alone; let us serve the Egyptians? Moses, recognizing that fear was distorting their memories and arousing their passions against him, sought to reassure them that the LORD would deliver them by fighting for them (cf. 15:3; Neh. 4:20; Ps. 35:1) as they remained firm in confidence. Surprisingly, as they came to their greatest moment of deliverance, the people of God were full of distrust and fear."[67]

I believe that Israel was an unstable group of people. When the hearts and minds of people are full of fear, it will cause a crisis every time. I contend that it takes a strong leader to navigate through the rough edges of uncertainty. If leaders in the church are going to be effective, they must learn how to deal with contention and faithless people. They must remind people of the faithfulness of God.

I believe that Moses was at his best under pressure. He assures Israel to "fear not, stand still and see the salvation of the Lord." How Moses handles the situation says something about his leadership skills and dependency upon God. Terry Thomas claims, "Moses response in this situation is crucial because the circumstances surrounding them were forcing the people to surrender their hope. This was their first real challenge toward their journey to the

---

[67] John Walvoord and Roy B. Zuck, *The Bible Knowledge Commentary: An Exposition of the Scriptures* (Wheaton, IL : Victor Books, 1983), 131.

Promised Land. In spite of the circumstance, the leader must always be ready to offer hope."[68] If the leaders in the church fail to give hope in hopeless situations, the people will became unstable and contentious. Thomas points out that Martin Luther King's, "leadership style was alive among the masses. Dr. King once stated, 'we must accept finite disappointment, but we must never lose infinite hope…Because when you lose hope you die …Basic in our philosophy [of preaching] is a deep faith in the future…Ours is a movement based on hope.' Dr. King realized that hope is a sustaining element, not only in leadership, but in life. Hope motivates and inspires. It causes people to take action."[69] It is through hope that leaders inspire the masses to move beyond their doubt and discontentment. It is a hope that inspires the masses to move in a positive and productive fashion. Terry Thomas has suggested that:

> When the people we lead express statements of discontentment because of facing what appears to be insurmountable challenge, we must respond to them with a message of hope, an extreme confidence in God's ability to handle the situation. I am aware that the Red Sea is before us and the mountains are all around us. I know that our men have no might against Pharaoh's army. However,

---

[68] Thomas. 45.
[69] Ibid.

God is my light, my rock, my high tower, my salvation. Then whom shall we fear? We are instructed 1 Peter 3:15 "[to] sanctify the Lord God in your hearts: and be ready always to give an answer to every man that asketh you a reason of the hope that is in you, with meekness and fear.[70]

As Moses reassures the people concerning God's divine protection, God parts the Red (Reed) Sea. God parts the sea in front of their enemies. In the midst of this, God established the leadership of Moses in the eyes of the people. God tells Moses in Exodus 14: 15-16, "Then the LORD said to Moses, 'Why are you crying out to me? Tell the Israelites to move on. Raise your staff and stretch out your hand over the sea to divide the water so that the Israelites can go through the sea on dry ground.'"[71] I assert that it is through the voice of the leader that followers gain a sense of hope in the midst of their hopeless situations. The leader must speak out to affirm what direction God is leading them. Silence is not the answer to lead people.

---

[70] Ibid.
[71] Exodus 14:15-16.

MOSES WAS CONFIDENT THAT GOD WOULD ESTABLISH HIS LEADERSHIP

Moses was an ideal leader in the Old Testament because he was confident that God would establish his leadership. It was after the first great event that God established the leadership of Moses. The people gained a greater trust and respect for God and Moses their leader. In Exodus 14:31, "And when the Israelites saw the great power the LORD displayed against the Egyptians, the people feared the LORD and put their trust in him and in Moses His servant."[72] God allows situations to happen in the life of the church/individual to bring about a total surrender unto Him. Israel had a great moment of discontentment and doubt about God and their leader but God turned their insurmountable challenges into a testimony for what God could do. Terry Thomas suggest that, "the manner in which a person respond to the initial statement of discontentment is a means in which a person's leadership begins to be established in the eyes of the people he or she has been appointed to lead. Therefore, if the people you lead are expressing their statements of discontentment to you that perhaps is a sign of their endorsement of your leadership. It is an indication that they

---

[72] Ibid.

perceive that you, as their leader, have the ability to resolve their statement of discontentment."[73] I contend that whenever the leader in the church faces discontentment in the crowd, he/she should respond with a message of hope and confidence that God will make a way.

These experiences and characteristics that Moses exemplified as a leader in the Old Testament were some great ones for leaders to follower. He was an ideal leader in the Old Testament because he was commissioned from God to lead God's people to a land flowing with milk and honey, and courageous enough to confront Pharaoh even though he felt insufficient. However, Moses was very effective as a leader because he was committed to God and offered hope to God's people in spite of the contention in the crowd. As a leader, he was confident that God would establish his leadership. I assert that Moses was an effective leader and leaders in the twenty first century should always be willing to model after such leadership because he brought about change in that particular paradigm.

---

[73] Thomas. 46.

CHAPTER III - THE "HOLY" CONNECTION IN THE OLD TESTAMENT

Fill in the blank

1. The contemporary church is comprised of all kinds of _____ _____.

2. The sad fact is that many leaders are _____ of the position that has been given to them.

3. Leadership in the local church is different from other _____ in our society.

4. The church is not an organization but an _____ that lives and gives birth to helping hurting humanity.

5. The Old Testament model contends that _____ was the most important and significant leader in the life of Israel.

6. _____ was commissioned by God to lead God's people to a land flowing with milk and honey.

7. _____ had the courage to confront the many challenges of dealing with Pharaoh, although he felt insufficient.

8. Moses was committed to God and offered _____ in spite of contention in the crowd.

9. Moses was confident that God would establish his _____.

10. God instructed Moses to take off his _____ as a sign of reverence.

Discussion Questions

1. Moses had leadership qualities and characteristics that made him an ideal leader in the Old Testament. Name the four and explain each one.

   _____
   _____
   _____
   _____
   _____
   _____

2. Where did Moses receive his calling?

   _____
   _____
   _____
   _____

3. Was Moses educated and trained to lead the people? Is this important in leadership today?

_____
_____
_____
_____
_____
_____

4. How important is it for a leader to have an encounter with God in order to liberate people around them?

_____
_____
_____
_____
_____
_____

5. Is it important for a leader to be courageous and committed in confronting the task before them? If so, please explain using Moses as an example.

_____
_____
_____
_____
_____
_____

CHAPTER IV

THE "HOLY" CONNECTION IN THE NEW TESTAMENT

The discussion of leadership concerning the contemporary church must begin with Jesus Christ who stated that, "that thou art Peter, and upon this rock I will build my church; and the gates of Hades shall not prevail against it." [74] Therefore, the discussion of leadership in the contemporary church begins with its creator and maker, Jesus Christ. Charles A. Tidwell points out that, "while no single passage of Scripture offers a comprehensive concept comparable to the Jethro Moses model, a study of the total approach of Jesus in relation to His apostles shows Him clearly in the roles preparing them to minister. He furnished them the essentials for performing ministry. He equipped them to do 'greater things that I am doing'(John 14:12)."[75] I contend that it is through the equipping of leaders to lead others that the church becomes stronger in what God is calling them to do. The New Testament shows the "Holy"

---

[74] Matthew 16:18.

[75] Charles A. Tidwell, *Church Administration: Effective Leadership for Ministry* (Nashville, Tennessee: Boardman Press., 1985), 41.

connection leadership of Jesus in his love for missions and being an example before the people.

NEW TESTAMENT MODEL

Jesus achieved his mission by preaching, teaching, healing, and giving of Himself. I will explore each of these principles that Jesus exemplified as a leader.

Jesus preached about the kingdom of God. Stephen Harris in *The New Testament: A Student's Introduction* points out that Jesus attempted to convey his vision of God's kingdom and how it would impact the world.[76] The English phrase "kingdom of God" translates the Greek expression *basileia tou theou. Basileia* refers primarily to the act or process of ruling, a quality or privilege that distinguishes a king or other ruler. It is to process control, freedom, and independence. Jesus showed his control, freedom, and independence through his preaching. According to Harris, "the biblical God who infinite kingship Israel's thinkers take for granted, has these attributes in abundance."[77]

---

[76] Stephen L. Harris. *The New Testament: A Student's Introduction* 3rd ed.(Mountain View, California: Mayfield Publishing Company, 1999), 227.
[77] Ibid.

Jesus is pictured using *basileia tou theou* in four major ways: (1) to express the kingdom preeminence; (2) to defend his personal authority to represent the kingdom and interpret the divine will; (3) to imply the nature of his self-awareness—the view he holds about his relationship with God and the meaning of kingship; (4) to proclaim the kingdom's radical demand for total commitment.[78] Throughout the Synoptic Gospel, the kingdom of God appears to dominate the message of Jesus. For example, in the Sermon on the Mount, Matthew presents Jesus giving high priority to the kingdom of God. The disciple who put God's kingdom and his righteousness first will receive an abundance of blessing (Matt. 6:33). I believe that the black church thrives on good preaching. Preaching that is transformative will focus on the kingdom of God. If Jesus preached about the kingdom of God, it is the task of the preacher to preach the message that Jesus preached. I contend that the church must rally around the preaching hour because it is what changes lives and offers hope.

---

[78] Ibid.

JESUS ACHIEVED HIS MISSION BY TEACHING

Jesus achieved his mission by teaching. In the four gospels, Jesus was recognized as someone who taught with great authority. " Jesus went throughout Galilee, teaching in their synagogues, preaching the good news of the kingdom, and healing every disease and sickness among the people. News about him spread all over Syria, and people brought to him all who were ill with various diseases, those suffering severe pain, the demon-possessed, those having seizures, and the paralyzed, and he healed them. Large crowds from Galilee, the Decapolis,[a] Jerusalem, Judea, and the region across the Jordan followed him," (Matthew 4:23-25).[79] Jesus allowed his teaching to impact the masses versus the masses impacting him. His teaching helped the masses to discover their purpose and plan for their lives. I assert that leaders need to be taught. It is impossible to teach what you don't know and lead where you don't go. According to Matthew 5-7, Jesus was teaching about the beatitudes and "the crowd was amazed at his teaching" (7:28). In Matthew 7:29, "he was one who taught with authority." In the gospel of Luke, Jesus did a lot of teaching

---

[a] That is, the Ten Cities
[79] Matthew 4:23-25.

and healing (16:16-18, 6:17-19, 14:7-14) to name a few. In the gospel according to Mark, Jesus arrives in home town teaching in the synagogue (6:1). Terry Thomas in his book, *Becoming a Fruit-Bearing Disciple,* asserts that "Jesus disciples did not focus on learning his words, but they focused on learning his lifestyle. Alyce M. Mckenzie says in her book, *Hear and Be wise Becoming a Preacher and Teacher of Wisdom,* that to be disciples of Jesus one must listen to his words and also observe his life."[80] In watching Jesus heal the sick, raise the dead, pray, worship, teach, cast out demons, and endure suffering his followers learned a lot by just watching Jesus. I contend that if the church is going to develop leaders, they must follow the teaching examples of Jesus as well as His lifestyle. Leadership must be concerned about the teaching ministry of the church, its practices and set out to live a life that is worth following.

Guns points out that there must be two levels in the teaching ministry of the church.

> First, we must be concerned about what is taught. Does what we teach enrich and increase spiritual growth and ministry effectiveness? What is taught in church or in training sessions must make a real difference in the lives of people and in the life of the church. Second, we must be concerned

---

[80] Terry Thomas, *Becoming a Fruit-Bearing Disciple* (Raleigh, North Carolina: Voice of Rehoboth, 2005), 68.

about who is teaching. What is the level of knowledge, personal character and public reputation of the teacher? The ministry of teaching is a spiritual gift given to the church for the purpose of building up the church for work of ministry (see Romans 12:7; 1 Corinthians 12:28-29; Ephesians 4:11; 1 John 3:1).[81]

Jesus lived a life that matters. His teaching was followed by His lifestyle. He was a man given too much prayer and devotion to God. If the church leaders are going to be relevant in this century there needs a strong emphasis on teaching and living a life that matters. It is through teaching that we equip the saints for ministry. Jesus stated in the great commission, "Therefore go and make disciples of all nations, baptizing them in the name of the Father and of the Son and of the Holy Spirit, and teaching them to obey everything I have commanded you. And surely I am with you always, to the very end of the age." [82] The importance of teaching will help the believer to understand the commands that Jesus has left for us to do. If you can teach them, then I believe you can lead them. Leaders in the church must be present and alert when an opportunity is presented to them to learn from a teaching moment about their responsibilities as a leader.

---

[81] Guns, 48.
[82] Matthew 28:18-20.

JESUS ACHIEVED HIS MISSION BY HEALING

Jesus achieved his mission by healing. During Jesus' earthly ministry, the world was full of people who needed healing from their brokenness and Jesus met their needs. William R. Herzog II in *Prophet and Teacher: An Introduction to the Historical Jesus* points that "Jesus was a traditional healer who was interested in healing both illness and disease. Disease refers to what is physically wrong with a person (e.g., leprosy) while illness refers to the social consequences of the disease (e.g., isolation, being cut off from friends and family). This explains why Jesus' exorcisms and healing so often lead to the restoration of those who have been healed."[83] I assert that the healing of the mind is also a part of healing. The mind is at peace once it has been taught. Paul said, "Therefore, I urge you, brothers, in view of God's mercy, to offer your bodies as living sacrifices, holy and pleasing to God—this is your spiritual [a] act of worship. Do not conform any longer to the pattern of this world, but be transformed by the renewing of your mind. Then you will be able to test and approve what

---

[83] William R. Herzog II. *Prophet and Teacher: An Introduction to the Historical Jesus* (Louisville, Kentucky: Westminster John Knox Press, 2005), 87.
   [a] Or *reasonable*

God's will is—his good, pleasing and perfect will. [84] I contend that the minds of the leaders have to be transformed in order for them to bring about transformation in the lives of others. They can be transformed by renewing it every day in God's word. The leadership in the church must receive healing of mind, body, and soul. There are many miracles that Jesus did to help the hurting and the disenfranchised that leaders must keep in mind. For example in Mark 5:1-6 it states:

> "They went across the lake to the region of the Gerasenes.[a] ² When Jesus got out of the boat, a man with an evil[b] spirit came from the tombs to meet him. ³ This man lived in the tombs, and no one could bind him anymore, not even with a chain. ⁴ For he had often been chained hand and foot, but he tore the chains apart and broke the irons on his feet. No one was strong enough to subdue him. ⁵ Night and day among the tombs and in the hills he would cry out and cut himself with stones. ⁶ When he saw Jesus from a distance, he ran and fell on his knees in front of him. ⁷ He shouted at the top of his voice, "What do you want with me, Jesus, Son of the Most High God? Swear to God that you won't torture me!" ⁸ For Jesus had said to him, "Come out of this man, you evil spirit!" ⁹ Then

---

[84] *New International Version*, electronic ed. (Grand Rapids: Zondervan, 1996, c1984), Ro 12:1-2.
[a] Some manuscripts *Gadarenes*; other manuscripts *Gergesenes*
[b] Greek *unclean*; also in verses 8 and 13

Jesus asked him, "What is your name?" "My name is Legion," he replied, "for we are many." [10] And he begged Jesus again and again not to send them out of the area. [11] A large herd of pigs was feeding on the nearby hillside. [12] The demons begged Jesus, "Send us among the pigs; allow us to go into them." [13] He gave them permission, and the evil spirits came out and went into the pigs. The herd, about two thousand in number, rushed down the steep bank into the lake and were drowned. [14] Those tending the pigs ran off and reported this in the town and countryside, and the people went out to see what had happened. [15] When they came to Jesus, they saw the man who had been possessed by the legion of demons, sitting there, dressed and in his right mind; and they were afraid. [16] Those who had seen it told the people what had happened to the demon-possessed man—and told about the pigs as well."[85]

It is clear in these verses that Jesus mission was to heal those who were disenfranchised. The man in the text needed the healing and delivering hand from Jesus and he granted unto him. According to Herzog, "The healing vouches for Jesus as a reliable and powerful broker of Yahweh's forgiveness of sin and cancellation of debt..., Jesus is no longer just a disputant. He is a force to be reckoned with, a shamanistic figure and broker who

---

[85]Mark 5:1-16

mediates power. He is a public, political presence who cannot be ignored or snubbed in the hope that he will wither and go away. The healing is, therefore, a necessary part of the incident, not just an add-on, but how Jesus healed and just exactly what the man's malady was can no longer be known."[86] If the church of today would follow the examples of Jesus' healing, we would have more healing of mind, body, and soul. I assert that leaders in the church must equip others to the knowledge of Christ's amazing power. Leadership can reference other passages where Christ shows his healing power, such as (Mark 5:35-42; John 11:38-44; Matthew 4:23-25). The model that He set forth is a good example of leadership in a socio-evangelical ministry. It is my belief that leadership must address the healing aspects of Jesus to a hurting world for we are all wounded healers.

CHRIST WAS A SERVANT

As a leader, he was a perfect model for all to follow. Christ taught his disciples what true greatness was all about. Terry Thomas points out, "Jesus used the description of a servant to identify himself to his disciples.

---

[86] Herzog, 87.

Perhaps the most descriptive identification of a disciple of Jesus is that of being a servant. Jesus even encouraged and admonished his disciples to aspire to become a servant."[87] Mark's gospel points out that:

> They came to Capernaum. When he was in the house, he asked them, 'What were you arguing about on the road?' But they kept quiet because on the way they had argued about who was the greatest. Sitting down, Jesus called the Twelve and said, 'If anyone wants to be first, he must be the very last, and the servant of all.' He took a little child and had him stand among them. Taking him in his arms, he said to them, 'Whoever welcomes one of these little children in my name welcomes me; and whoever welcomes me does not welcome me but the one who sent me.'[88]

Christ's lessons on greatness teaches us that the one "who is the greatest is the servant." It is my belief that there must be more servants in the church. Servants that have a mind like Christ, a mind that is concerned for the young and the old. Guns points out that Robert K. Greenleaf's ideas about servant leadership which came from reading Hermann Hesse's *Journey to the East* is a good example of servant leadership. He wrote that:

---

[87] Thomas, 81
[88] Mark 9:33-37.

In this story, we see a band of men on a mythical journey, probably also Hesse's own journey. The central figure of the story is Leo, who accompanies the party as the servant who does their menial chores, but who also sustains them with his spirit and his song. He is a person of extraordinary presence. All goes well until Leo disappears. The group falls into disarray and the journey is abandoned. They cannot make it without the servant Leo. The narrator, one of the parties, after some years of wandering, finds that Leo is taken into the order that had sponsored the journey. There he discovers that Leo, whom he had known first as servant, was in fact the titular head of the Order, its guiding spirit, a great and noble leader."[89]

I assert that in order for us to be great leaders we have to be servants first, not self-serving. Jesus was a servant leader. He took on the menial tasks and stooped to do the jobs that no one else would do. Greenleaf remarked, "The great leader is seen as servant first, and that simple fact is the key to his greatness.[90]" A great example of the servant spirit that Jesus presented to his followers can be seen in John13:4-17 during the Passover. Prior to his crucifixion, Jesus washes their feet. He uses that as a teaching moment for the disciples to understand that washing each other's feet is a sign of great humility. Guns point out that:

---

[89] Guns, 53.
[90] Ibid.

> The point of the washing was two-fold. First, Jesus wanted to demonstrate to His disciples what it meant to be a servant. Definitions are fine, but living examples are clearer. Second, when Jesus washed their feet, it was a symbol of spiritual cleaning. Every leader within the church must examine their spirituality. Am I doing the things necessary to develop and maintain a committed and close relationship with the Lord? If you and I expect to be Christ like leaders, we must possess a spirit of humility and service."[91]

It is interesting to note that washing of the feet was also vital in that custom. The feet were the most disgusting part of the body because it was in contact with all elements. Terry Thomas points out that:

> In spite of that, Jesus humbled himself and became a servant to his disciples. Washing feet was not Jesus' responsibility. Jesus was teacher and master. In principle...the rabbis' students were to learn the torah, not only from the teaching of the master, but also from daily contact with him. Concretely, daily contact meant that they waited on their master as his personal servants. The rule was that the knowledge of the Torah could not be gained without service to the experts.[92]

It is my belief that servant hood is the hallmark of a great servant. It is when leaders serve those whom God has

---

[91] Ibid.54.
[92] Thomas, 82

sent them. The church must focus on how it can become greater servants for Christ. If leadership would focus on servanthood, it would bring about an everlasting change in the church. In conclusion, Jesus was an ideal leader in the New Testament because He showed his leadership skill by developing the mission through preaching, teaching, healing, and being a model servant.

He is the perfect model for the New Testament church to follow. Terry Thomas in *an Exploration into the Task of Leadership* is correct when he states, "leadership is needed in the church because of needs that are yet to be met. The church needs person who can envision how unmet needs can be met, the tenacity to make it a reality and the foresight of needs that will develop in the future, subsequently having the church ready to meet those needs when they arise."[93] I believe that these needs can be met through strong leadership and the power of Him who has sent us.

---

[93] Thomas, 2.

CHAPTER IV - THE "HOLY" CONNECTION IN THE NEW TESTAMENT

Fill in the blank

1. The discussion of leadership concerning the contemporary church must being with _____ — who stated that "thou art Peter and upon this rock I will build my church."

2. Jesus achieved his mission by

   _____

   _____ and
   _____ of himself.

3. Jesus preached about _____.

4. The English phrase _____ refers primarily to the act or process of ruling, equality or privilege that distinguishes a king or other ruler.

5. Jesus is pictured using the Kingdom of God in four major ways:
   - _____
   - _____
   - _____
   - _____

6. Throughout the _____
   the Kingdom of God appears to dominate the
   message of Jesus.

7. _____ that is
   transformative will focus on the Kingdom of God.

8. Jesus achieved his mission by
   _____.

9. Jesus allowed his teaching to impact the
   _____ versus the
   _____ impacting him.

10. Jesus disciples did not focus on learning his words,
    they focused on learning his
    _____.

Answer **True** or **False**

1. ____ It is through teaching that we equip the saints for ministry.
2. ____ The importance of teaching will help the believer to understand the commands that Jesus has left for us to do.
3. ____ Jesus was a traditional healer who was interested in healing both ills and diseases for charge.

4. _____ Diseases refer to what is physically wrong with a person while ills refer to a social consciousness of the disease, such as isolation, depression, etc.

5. _____ The mind is at peace once it has been taught the Word of God.

6. _____ As a leader, Jesus was a perfect model for all to follow.

7. _____ Christ lesson on greatness teaches us that the one who is the least is the servant.

8. _____ In order to be a great leader servants first must not be self-serving.

9. _____ Jesus took on menial tasks and stooped to do the jobs that no one else would do.

10. _____ A great example of the servant spirit that Jesus presented to his followers can be seen during the Passover prior to him being crucified; Jesus washed their feet.

CHAPTER V

THE "HOLY" CONNECTION

Historically church fathers have seen the need for leadership in the church. According to Lovett H. Weems, Jr., "From its beginning the church has recognized the need for some person to be set apart for leadership of the community. The church father Jerome put it, 'there can be no church community without a leader or team of leaders.' Theologian Annie Janbert reminds us that in the earliest Christian communities leadership was seen as 'the responsibility of all and the charge of some.'"[94] Strong leadership has been the key to developing and maintaining a healthy church. In the midst of this, church leaders have seen the need to develop and evaluate their leadership skills and abilities as they lead others. Hippolytus of Rome (A.D. 170-236), according to Gerald L. Sittser author of *Water from a Deep Well,* "wrote *On the Apostolic Tradition* in A.D. 215 to provide a manual that instructed bishops and presbyters about how to teach new believers the essential of the faith. The period of instruction lasted up to three years. Amazingly, most of the church fathers—Origen, John Chrysostom, Augustine of Hippo, Theophilus of Jerusalem,

---

[94] Lovett H. Weems, Jr. *Church Leadership: Vision, Team, Culture, and Integrity* (Nashville, Tn.: Abingdon Press: 1993), 27.

for example—taught those classes, demonstrating that instruction of new believers was so important that only the best-trained pastors were qualified to take on the responsibility."[95]

Training has been an ongoing process. I assert that leadership has to realize that if they are going to be effective they must prepare themselves for the leadership. The time has passed when assuming you know and don't know is gone. The pews are crying out for leadership. There are new paradigms and ideas that have been brought on by a changing world. David A. Ramey asserts,

> The quest for lifelong learning is integral to the process of developing leaders. Leaders are measured not in the knowledge or expertise they possess, but in their capacity to learn from the unknown, the unexpected, and the unexplored. The task of leadership requires the courage of conviction to venture beyond our comfort zone of existing knowledge and experience to discover new and alternative ways of thinking, acting, and behaving to lift our organization and ourselves to greater levels of accomplishment.[96]

---

[95] Gerald L. Sittser, *Water from a Deep Well* (Downers Grove, IL: InterVarsity Press: 2007), 66.

[96] David A. Ramey, *Empowering the Leaders* (Kansas City, Missouri: Sheed & Ward, 1991), 94.

It is my belief that leadership training is the key to an effective organization. Terry Thomas gives an excellent definition concerning leadership when he states that leadership is, "mobilizing people to move from a state beneath their God given potentiality while guiding them to a position of promise and possibility whereby their potentiality can be actualized. This position of promise and possibility, I might add, is a place designated by God. In other words, pastoral/laity leadership or Christian leadership is guiding a congregation or individual to their Promised Land."[97] It is imperative that leaders see the potential in the people that they lead. I believe that the potential to see the greatness in people and cultivate that greatness is leadership. A good example is the desert saint, Antony of Egypt. St. Antony was known as one who would cultivate persons for the ministry. Sittser points out, "he became an adviser to hundreds who hoped to achieve the spiritual depth he exhibited, whom he exhorted to die daily, discard their possessions and prepare themselves for the Day of Judgment."[98] The leadership in the church must see in people greatness even though they don't see it. Leaders must equip others for greatness in order for greatness to

---

[97] Thomas, 38.
[98] Sittser, 77.

come forth. Terry Thomas asserts that, "a leader must see the possibilities that lie within the people they lead. Wayne Cordeiro says that when he looks at the forest he see more than trees. He sees houses, beautiful dressers, rocking chairs, bed frames, cabinets and desks! They're all in the forest, and they are beautiful!."[99] It is Cordeiro's belief that we must view the people that we lead in the same manner. It is also Cordeiro's position that we see the potential and possibilities in the people we lead. He explained:

> No, you won't find them already completed. But the potential is all there. Sure, you'll still have to cut and sand and varnish the wood, but it's all there. Everything you need to furnish your entire home is in that forest. You just need to see more than trees in order to be motivated to harvest the wood. You have to see their potential! You gotta believe that there's gold in the hills if you're gonna muster up the energy you need to mine it out.[100]

Historically, leadership training was important for leaders to develop and maintain a level of training to keep leaders on task and relevant in their particular church. This book will explore this by explaining leadership historically by examining:

---

[99] Ibid., 38.
[100] Ibid.

(1) How biblical leaders used effective administrative skills to bring about change.

(2) How post biblical leaders equipped others to lead.

HISTORICALLY IN DEVELOPING LEADERSHIP

Historically in developing leadership, there has been a need in equipping the leaders for administrative skills so that they can become more effective. Strong administrative skills have been one of the components in developing strong leaders. Charles A. Tidwell points out that, "church leaders need to discover, accept, and develop an administrative style of leadership. The need is not a new one. Neither is the approach to the remedy. Both are apparent in history at least as far back as the Exodus."[101] Moses is a perfect example and will be discussed later in the book. However, leaders must keep in mind that it is impossible for one leader to carry the load for everyone. History shows that leaders must surround themselves with people in whom they can equip for the ministry.

I contend that equipping leaders to lead others in an excellent model to follow because the burden of leadership is not on one person. However, leaders must sharpen their

---

[101] Tidwell, 17.

administrative skills as they are equipped to do ministry. When leaders are equipped in the ministry, they can help the ministry to strive and face the many challenges before it. There must be an active equipping ministry in the church to bring about effective change. Joe Ellis in the *Church on Purpose* points out that, "Elton Trueblood was among the first to raise the current emphasis on the idea of an equipping ministry. He describes the congregation as a team in which every member is responsible for helping attain the goal. The minister functions as a player-coach, whose job it is to train and lead the team to victory-not a sideline coach, but a playing coach right alongside all the other team members."[102] It is imperative that the leader places more emphasis on people than things. I believe that when the emphasis is on things it breaks down the communication that would bring about effectiveness. It is strange enough to realize that many church leaders don't communicate and relate well with people. Tidwell points out that, "studies by seminary curriculum committees and others continue to show that the biggest problem area for church leaders, specifically ministers, is their inability to relate satisfactorily and effectively to people."[103] In leading

---

[102] Joe S. Ellis, *The Church On Purpose: Key to Effective Church Leadership* (Cincinnati, Ohio: Standard Publishing. 1982), 56.
[103] Tidwell, 35.

people, I contend that the church leaders must develop his or her administrative skills in working with people. In order to equip them, leaders must learn how to be in relationship with them and communicate with them effectively in order to lead them. Ellis assets, "equipping is a dynamic, purpose-oriented concept. It means, 'furnishing or preparing someone for service or action.'"[104] The equipping ministry concept aligns the focus and purpose of the ministry. Ellis asserts that, "the equipping concept adjusts the focus of ministry. A minister who seeks to equip his people for service is not merely a Chaplain who renders service to his clients. He works to enable other Christians to achieve God's purposes."[105] The equipping ministry has been a vital part of all successful ministries. For an example Sittser point out,

> By the middle of the second century, pastors were already following an established liturgy of worship. On Sunday they called believers together for worship, which was usually held in large homes. They read from the memoirs of the apostles, preached a sermon and led the church in singing and corporate prayers. Then they distributed the bread and wine to the faithful. They also collected funds and appointed deacons to distribute those funds and thus provided 'for the orphans and widows, those who are in need on account of

---

[104] Ellis, 56.
[105] Ibid.

sickness or some other cause, those who are in bonds, strangers who are sojourning.' The deacons became the protector of all who are in needed.[106]

Historically, it has been the equipping of others that has made the difference. The historical leadership models of Jethro-Moses and Jesus are excellent biblical models on how they equipped other to do the work of the ministry. I would like to explain each of these models historically and how they equipped leaders to lead others.

JETHRO-MOSES LEADERSHIP MODEL

There are several biblical models that we can learn from regarding the equipping ministry concept. Each one of the models has a unique concept toward good church administration. However, the Jethro-Moses Model is an excellent example of how Jethro shared with Moses how to equip the children of Israel so that their individual needs could be met. It was collaboration of leadership, a process of connections and systems. This was helpful because Moses was trying to handle each situation himself. Jethro boldly told him what he was doing was not good for the people. Tidwell stated that Jethro give him a prescription

---

[106] Sittser, 66.

for equipping ministry. Jethro asked that God's presence would be with Moses and the authoritative command of God persuaded Moses to listen to the voice of his father-in-law. Tidwell asserts these as the major points of the prescription for collaboration of leadership, a process of connections and systems. I would like to examine the nine processes of connections and systems. They are: pray for them, teach them the guidelines, show them the way, show them the work, organize the people into manageable groups, choose qualified men to lead each group, give the chosen leaders continuing authority, have leaders decide routine matters and bring great matters to the chief leader. These are major components in equipping leadership.

1. *Pray for them-* Moses was to seek God's face for the people. He was to bring their problems before God that God could heal them and deliver them.
2. *Teach them the guidelines-* He was to teach them the statutes and the laws. These were to be the guidelines, as policies, procedures, and rules.
3. *Show them the way-* He was to show them how they could live their lives. He was their spiritual counselor. Since God used a pillar of cloud and fire

for their physical direction, this admonition must refer to Moses showing them life direction.

4. ***Show them the work*** - Moses was to show the people the work that God had ordained for them to do. This work was a part of the redemptive purposes that God had outlined. It was God's way of challenging them to do a great work. It was to provide much of the motivation for their struggle to become the kind of instrument as a people through whom God could work.

5. ***Organize the people into manageable groups*** - Moses was to organize the people into groups so that they could be managed. He was to have the group of thousands, which in turn, would have groups of hundreds. The groups were sub-grouped into fifties, and the fifties into groups of ten. He developed an organizational plan so that every person's needs could be met.

6. ***Choose qualified men to lead each group*** - Moses was to see that qualified men were provided "out of all the people" to be placed over each unit of the organization suggested. The "job qualifications" are impressive. These leaders were to be able, God fearing, truthful, haters of unjust gain. Their span of

leadership was reasonable—each man could be expected to cover his assignment effectively.

7. ***Give the chosen leaders continuing authority-*** Moses was to let the chosen leaders of the group judge the people at all seasons. Their authority was not limited to any season. No one would benefit by waiting for a different season for his arbitration to be handled. This arrangement would expedite the solving of disputes and avoid a loaded docket. It would be an exception to the statutes and laws which would not be decided by these judges. This pinpointed responsibility both for the people and for their leaders.

8. ***Have leaders decide routine matters-*** Moses was to have the chosen judges to decide on the small matters and the larger matters were to be brought to him. The matters in which they solved where covered by statutes and laws or which were of limited magnitude. These kinds of problems were to be solved on the lowest possible level of the organizational structure—at the point nearest the problem itself—where the facts of the issues were most readily apparent.

9. ***Bring "great matters" to the chief leader-*** The great matters were to be brought to Moses so that he could handle them. These were matters that were not satisfactorily dealt with under the statues and the laws. Moses was to judge the exception that was not covered. He was to manage by exception, a management concept which has been articulated in this century by some as though they invented it.[107]

The wisdom that Jethro shared with Moses was insightful and beneficial to the children of Israel. It strengthened the organization of the ministry. I would assert that the plan helped the burden to be placed on everybody. It is important that the church focus on the equipping of others, so that the responsibilities of dealing with small issues are not placed on the chief leader. Too many responsibilities will overwhelm the chief leader (Pastor). The Jethro-Moses model, according to Tidwell, "would be easy to point out some untimely aspects of the Jethro-Moses in applying it to democratic leadership in a church. The times have afforded some changes in situational factors which would make some of the model unsuited to the church. But a model does not have to be a

---

[107] Tidwell, 39-40.

perfect model in order to be instructive."[108] The model that Jethro shared with Moses could be used to bring about suitable change and organization. I assert that it shows leadership how to develop a collaboration of leadership, a process of connections and systems by taking the load off of the chief leader and allowing leadership to be shared by those around the leader. It is a unique paradigm for the 21st century to follow. If the church is going to be effective in the 21st century, it must reexamine the way it does ministry.

JESUS LEADERSHIP MODEL

The model that Jesus used to equip the disciples for ministry is also an excellent model to examine. It is paramount that leaders look at some of the fundamental components that Jesus shared and exemplified with His followers. I would like to examine four aspects that Jesus modeled for equipping the disciples as leaders. The four aspects are:

(1) He spent most of His time with the disciples versus religious leaders.

---

[108] Ibid., 41.

(2) He spent a great deal of time training and equipping the disciples to equip others for ministry.

(3) He trained and showed them how to be effective servants to the people.

(4) The servant model the He used gave the disciple the tools to turn the world upside down.

JESUS SPENT MOST OF HIS TIME WITH THE DISCIPLES

Jesus spent most of his time with the disciples verses the religious leaders. Tidwell points out that the approach that Jesus used was very effective. He stated that William Hull gives the results and approach of Jesus by saying:

> When Jesus launched his ministry, he bypassed the religious professionals of his day, who lacked the training of the rabbis or the prestige of the priesthood, he said, "You are the salt of the earth, the light of the world," (see Matt. 5:13-16). It is astonishing how they became the pivot on which hung the very survival of his movement. It is not an exaggeration to say that when Jesus died he left only two things on earth-the blood split in loving sacrifice for others and the impact of his life upon a handful of frightened, faltering men. The fact that they were open to the reality of his resurrection, that they were willing to overcome provincialism in

carrying out a worldwide mission is testimony to the wisdom of the basic strategy Jesus followed.[109]

The equipping strategy of Jesus was so profound that it led to a massive growth in the church. I assert that the leadership of the church must spend time developing so that they may be able reach the masses. The twelve caught on to the concept very well and used it as an instrument to spread from being a tiny remnant with Judaism to become a worldwide faith. Hull asserts that, "…if the twelve had viewed themselves as the only legitimate ministers, they would soon have been overwhelmed as the group they led grew from 120 to three thousand at Pentecost. In fact, one might add that they very nearly were overwhelmed as the church grew, saved only by their administrative move to lead the church to choose others to share the work load with them (Acts 6)."[110] When Jesus equipped the disciples, he gave them the necessary tools to do a great work for the kingdom. I assert that if leadership in the church uses their tools effectively, they can change any given situation.

---

[109] Ibid., 42.
[110] Ibid.

JESUS SPENT A GREAT DEAL OF TIME TRAINING AND EQUIPPING THE DISCIPLES

Jesus spent a great deal of time training and equipping the disciples to equip others for the ministry. He said in the great commission, "all authority in heaven and on earth has been given to me. Therefore go and make disciples of all nations, baptizing them in the name of the Father and of the Son and of the Holy Spirit, and teaching them to obey everything I have commanded you. And surely I am with you always, to the very end of the age." [111] Making disciples was a part of equipping them. Jesus commanded his disciples to teach others what He had taught them. I believe that leadership should make other disciples for the kingdom. Leaders should be equipped and then equip others. Historically discipleship has been integral part of leadership development. Cartmill and Gentile in their book *Leadership Essentials* points out that, "Leadership skills are essential, but we are first called to be instruments of God who are guiding others toward spiritual growth and maturity. Not all disciples will be called into leadership roles, but let's be sure those who are leaders are grounded in the faith, building their leadership and ministry

---

[111] Matthew 28:16-20.

on the foundation of a growing relationship with God. In this way, we can better ensure the effectiveness of ministry, the self-care and development of the leader, and the care of those influenced by the leader."[112] It is my belief that discipleship training is a key component in developing the leadership of this church. I assert that when leadership in the church recognizes the importance and implements discipleship training into their daily lives, it will make a profound impact on those in whom they lead. As Jesus taught his followers, according to Tom Sine, discipleship was a call to be counter-cultural.[113] Sine goes on to say that, "In fact, if anything, his call to his disciples to be radically counter to the prevailing culture was dramatically pronounced. Jesus called his followers then as now not only to commit themselves to God and follow the way but also to transform radically their fundamental values and life priorities and commit themselves to be fulltime agents of the kingdom."[114] The training of leadership has been the key component for success in any organization. John Maxwell pointed out that, "leadership is developed daily, not in a day. That is the reality dictated by the Law of

---

[112] Carol Cartmill and Yvonne Gentile, *Leadership Essentials* (Nashville: Abingdon Press, 2006), 13.

[113] Tom Sine, *Taking Discipleship Seriously: a Radical Biblical Approach* (Valley Forge: Judson Press, 1985), 19.

[114] Ibid.

Process. Benjamin Disraeli asserted, 'the secret of success in life is for a man to be ready for his time when it comes'"[115] If leaders are going to be effective, there must be discipleship training. I believe that if leadership in the church takes discipleship training to heart, it can move the hearts of the people. Training should be at the top of every leader's agenda.

JESUS TRAINED AND SHOWED THE DISCIPLES HOW TO BE EFFECTIVE SERVANTS

Jesus trained and showed the disciples how to be effective servants to the people. In training the disciples on servant hood, Jesus would compare effective leadership and non-effective leadership. In Matthew 20:25-28, He compares the two by saying, "You know that the rulers of the Gentiles lord over them and their high officials exercise authority over them. Not so with you. Instead, whoever wants to become great among you must be your servant, and whoever wants to be first must be your slave—just as the Son of Man did not come to be served, but to serve, and to give his life as a ransom for many."[116] The custom was

---

[115] John C. Maxwell, *The 21 Irrefutable Laws of Leadership* (Nashville, Tn.: Thomas Nelson, 1998), 27.
[116] Matthew 20:25-29.

for their leaders to exercise authority down upon those under them. It was an authoritarian relationship between the leader and the follower. I believe that this type of leadership can cause more problems than solutions. The church must drop the ideology that leaders are superior to the followers. This can be seen in the way leaders treat their others, especially the new comers. In teaching His disciples, James and John assumed that Jesus' kingdom would have such an authority system and wanted to be in charge. These disciples did not grasp His kingdom agenda and the nature of leadership. Terry Thomas has suggested that "the highest aspiration of a disciple is to seek to become a servant to others. The ministry of a disciple of Jesus is not about status. It is not about setting at the head table. It is about serving others."[117] Jesus set forth a new paradigm for leadership. Ellis observation is similar to Thomas because he said that, "Jesus sets forth a relationship between leader and people in which servant-leadership is to prevail. The role is not one of authority but of service."[118] The servant leader model for leadership is to focus on the follower not the leader. Ellis goes on to say that, "Jesus discards once and for all secular ruler model for

---

[117] Thomas, 82.
[118] Ellis, 130.

His people and replaces it with a relationship that He himself first exemplified. Such a leader is a facilitator-enabler-equipper; his role is that of helping the body of people become functional in achieving their purposes."[119] I assert that leadership in the church must be about enabling others to develop and find their purpose. This has been absent from the present leadership.

THE SERVANT MODEL THAT JESUS EXEMPLIFIED GAVE THE DISCIPLES THE TOOLS

The servant model that Jesus exemplified gave the disciples the tools that they need to turn the world upside down. The servant leader, according to Ellis, "helps the body of people perceive their goals, develop commitment to them, mobilize to reach them, and pursue their achievement. He offers guidance, inspiration, instruction, and resources; but he strives to work in cooperation with the group as a team."[120] The servant-leader model that Jesus exemplified helped the disciples to make more disciples and turn the world upside down. I believe that the church can turn this community upside down if it would follow the

---

[119] Ibid., 131.
[120] Ibid.

model in which Jesus exemplified. He called them to be fishers of men. Ken Blanchard and Phil Hodges in the *Servant Leader* asserts that striving to be a servant leader, "you must elevate the growth and development of people from a 'means' goal to an 'end' goal of equal importance to the product or service mission of the organization. Servant Leadership requires a level of intimacy with the needs and aspirations of the people being led that might be beyond the level of intimacy an ego-driven leader is willing to sustain."[121] Blanchard and Hodges go on to say that, "servant leadership begins with a clear and compelling vision of the future that excites passion in the leader and commitment in those who follow. In practical terms a good vision has three parts; your purpose/mission: What business you are in- How will you benefit your customers?, Your preferred picture of the future: Where you are going- what will you look like if everything is running as planned?, Your values: How you want people to behave when they are working on your mission and picture of the future- What do you stand for?"[122] Jesus exemplified these characteristics before his disciples so that they could be fishers of men. I assert that if the church would see beyond

---

[121] Ken Blanchard and Phil Hodges, *the Servant Leader* (Nashville, Tn.: J. Countryman, 2003), 58.
[122] Ibid, 45.

the church walls and see the great harvest that God has laid before it, it can become a greater church.

The leadership must have the purpose, picture, and vision of the future; this happened when leaders hung around Jesus. The disciples hung around Jesus and his characteristics rubbed off on them. Terry Thomas asserts that "it is a known fact that if you hang around a person long enough you will find yourself unknowingly mimicking that person's behavior. Without thought or practice, our behavior begins to reflect the person or persons with whom we constantly share our time. Jessie Jackson claims that if you tell him who your friends are, he will be able to tell you what you are like."[123] I assert that if leadership builds a relationship with Christ, they too can turn the world upside down and make a difference in the world in which we live. It is Jesus' nature to change people who come into contact with him.

Although Jesus modeled the servant leader model, many of the early followers viewed him differently. Michael Coogan points out that, "Considering the number of messianic views prevalent in the first-century Jewish culture, Jesus would have evoked a variety of responses, even from those who knew him. Some saw him as a

---

[123] Thomas, 78.

political figure who would liberate the land from the Romans; some perhaps saw him as a priest who would restore the Temple; some saw him as a prophet and others as a sage; still others saw him as the promised return of Elijah or the new Moses. Some first-century Jews may well have regarded Jesus as a divine figure (for example, Wisdom incarnate), others as a human being divinely anointed."[124] The servant leader model that Jesus exemplified was an excellent example for church leaders to follow in spite of what other religious views thought. This model shows leaders how Jesus equipped the twelve for effective and relevant ministry during that time. I believe that it can make a difference in the church.

The leadership model that Jesus exemplified is a great model for the 21st century leaders to follow. It is a unique paradigm for leaders to follow if they desire to bring about relevant change. In observation, Jesus spent most of His time with the disciples verses the religious leaders and used a great deal of that time training and equipping them to equip others. Jesus showed them how to be effective servant leaders to the people by being a servant leader himself which in turn gave the disciples the tools that they needed to turn the world upside down. These are the

---

[124] Coogan, 374.

fundamental tools one needs to equip others to do relevant ministry in the 21st century.

POST- BIBLICAL LEADERS EQUIPPING OTHERS

The equipping of church leaders has been the bed rock of the Christian church. The Christian church has been able to with stand the heretics and pagan culture that surround its doors because of strong leadership. The post biblical church leaders like Origen, Augustine of Hippo, Martin Luther and Martin Luther King, Jr. to name a few, were instrumental in equipping others to defend their faith and prepare for the Christian ministry.

ORIGEN WAS A LEADER IN THE POST-BIBLICAL ERA

Origen was a leader in the post-biblical era who stressed the importance of equipping those who were in pastoral ministry. Sitter pointed out Origen wrote, "a pastor was called to function as a teacher, guide, a friend for the members of the flock, the great third-century teacher. The pastor's work depended on setting a good example or demonstrating 'perfection' (maturity of faith), for how could a pastor nurture in others what was lacking in his own life? There is no moral progress without the person of the spiritual helper, without the living example and loving participation of someone who is perfect."[125] It is clear that Origen saw the need in pastors being well equipped to lead others. However, Mark Ellingsen points out that Origen and Tertullian, "forbade a women to speak in the church, as in the Pauline literature."[126] I strongly disagree with their views concerning women to speak in church. The church has to be open for all classes, sexes, and races. It is vital that the leadership of the church see the importance of pastoral leadership being trained and equipped to enable those around them in ministry regardless of their plight. The fourth-century bishop, Gregory of Nazianzus, stated, "a man must himself be cleaned before cleansing others; himself become wise, that he may make others wise; become light, and then give light; draw near to God, and so bring others near."[127]

---

[125] Sittser, 66.

[126] Mark Ellingsen, *Reclaiming Our Roots: An Inclusive Introduction to Church History Volume 1 The Late First Century to the Eve of the Reformation* (Harrisburg, Pennsylvania; Trinity Press International, 1999), 45.

[127] Sittser, 66.

AUGUSTINE OF HIPPO EQUIPPED OTHER LEADERS

Augustine of hippo equipped other leaders by giving them sound advice about the ministry. He offered some advice on how to preach and teach by claiming "that the technique of teaching and communication (i.e., rhetoric) are advantageous only when God uses them. For God could give the gospel to humankind without human agency."[128] Augustine offered advice in response to various matters of discipline or turmoil in the churches. He claims that "it its best to honor local customs when there are no prescriptions by Scripture and Tradition. When addressing congregational sloth, Augustine asserts that it is good if pastors receive honor, but they ought not exult in it."[129] It is clear that Augustine is giving sound advice to those leaders during that era. Leaders in the church must be open to sound advice as well if they are going to be transformed. Sittser points how Augustine equipped other pastors and leaders during his era. He stated that:

---

[128] Mark Ellingsen, *The Richness of Augustine: His Contextual & Pastoral Theology* (Louisville, Kentucky; Westminster John Knox Press, 2005), 117.

[129] Ibid., 118.

As a bishop he organized a quasi- monastic community for pastors of the church. He sketched a rule for monasteries too, though not by intention. While serving as bishop he wrote a letter to a group of women whose nunnery was being torn apart by dissension. In the letter Augustine outlined principles that a community should follow if it hopes to be healthy. Like Basil, he believed that living with others is necessary for the cultivation of spiritual maturity, for life in community provides the best- in fact, the only—setting in which the most important of all virtues can be formed, and that is the virtue of love.

Perfection in the spiritual life is impossible to attain as long as a person lives alone, for how can that person learn how to love? Over time this 'Rule of St. Augustine', as it came to be called, was adapted to a variety of setting. [130]

I believe that leadership of the church must adhere to some of these great truths to strengthen the overall church. There must be principles (from the Bible) that will cultivate spiritual maturity of the church. Discipleship training and leadership training must continue to bring about a great change in the church.

---

[130] Sittser, 105.

MARTIN LUTHER EQUIPPED OTHERS IN THE MINISTRY

Martin Luther equipped others in the ministry through teaching and preaching. He was one of the great reformers of his time. While at Wittenberg, Luther discovered a new profound scripture that changed his life. The scripture was Romans 1:17 that talks about the righteousness of God which lead to his great transformation as a monk. Luther stated:

> This immediately made me feel as though I had been born again and as though I had entered through open gates into paradise itself. From that moment, I saw the whole face of Scripture in a new light... And now, where I once hated the phrase, 'the righteousness of God,' I began to love and extol it as the sweetest of phases, so that this passage in Paul became the very gate of paradise to me.

After this great awaking in the life of Luther, he began teaching Scripture to the faculty and students in Wittenberg, winning them over to his point of view. As he equipped others to his way of thinking, "he also began to challenge abuses in the church, such as the sale of indulgences, which popes dispensed in order to reduce the number of years the faithful had to spend in purgatory."[131] Out of his frustration and faith, On October 31, 1517 he posted the ninety-five page thesis that challenged the indulgences of the church and challenged them for a debate. Mark Ellingsen points how Luther was instrumental in equipping women for ministry. He stated that "Luther's general concern about the status of women is evident in his advocacy of education for girls as well as boys. His interaction with women's issues also took the form of reflections on their role as leaders in the church"[132] I believe that the church must be advocates for those who are without a voice, like women, children and the less fortunate.

MARTIN LUTHER KING, JR. WAS INSTRUMENTAL IN EQUIPPING OTHERS

Martin Luther King, Jr. was instrumental in equipping others to lead a great movement against segregation. In 1955 when a well-respected African American working woman refused to give up her set on a

---

[131] Sittser, 216.

[132] Mark Ellingsen, *Reclaiming Our Roots An Inclusive Introduction to Church History Volume II from Martin Luther to Martin Luther King Jr.* (Harrisburg, Pennsylvania; Trinity Press International. 1999), 49.

segregated bus, it led to a movement to protest segregation. Martin Luther King, Jr. was cast into the leadership role. Ellingsen points out that King, "was cast into the leadership of an eventually successful bus boycott by African Americans in the community. Later sit-ins and marches in Montgomery, Birmingham, Selma, Greensboro (involving students of North Carolina A &T), and finally Washington succeeded in exerting enough political pressure to bring about a civil rights bill and the eventual end of legalized segregation. On the way, King's vigorous advocacy of nonviolent resistance led to his receiving the coveted Nobel Peace Prize."[133] King was a great leader and motivator of the masses. I believe that leadership of the church must motivate the masses to do a great work for God. The only way they will move is through motivation. During the National Baptist Convention, Martin Luther King Jr. led a group of leaders to start a new convention over the validity of J.H. Jackson's presidency. Ellingsen points out, "these animosities, exacerbated by another dispute about the next election of the convention's president, as well as the conflicts over the best civil rights strategy, led King and many of his admirers to leave the convention and form the

---

[133] Ibid., 360.

Progressive National Baptist Convention in 1961."[134] I believe that the leadership in the church must see beyond the animosity of a few and lead others to a place where they can help utilize their God given potential.

HISTORICALLY THE CHALLENGE THAT HAS COME FROM CHANGE

In conclusion, historically the challenge that has come from change has caused some discontentment in the people. The discontentment is an indicator that change is taking place. In the midst of their discontentment, it shows a sign of unbelief in the Creator. This is often called a "crisis of unbelief." If change is going to be effective, there must be people in leadership that can manage that change and the conflict that it may bring. Historically, in dealing with the challenges that comes from change, leadership has seen the need to be equipped to manage conflict.

---

[134] Ibid., 361.

CHAPTER V - THE "HOLY" CONNECTION
Answer True or False.

1. ____ Historically church fathers have seen the need for leadership in the church.
2. ____ There can be no church community without a leader or team leader.
3. ____ Weak leadership has been the key to developing and maintaining a healthy church.
4. ____ Training leaders has to be an one time process.
5. ____ It's okay to assume you know and don't know, nobody will find out.
6. ____ The pew is crying out for leadership.
7. ____ The leader in a context must see in people greatness even though they cannot see it.
8. ____ Historically leadership training was not important for leaders to develop and maintain a level of training to keep leaders on task and relevant in their particular context.
9. ____ The position of promise and possibility is a place designated by God.
10. ____ It is imperative that leaders see the bad in people they are leading.

CHAPTER VI

THE "HOLY" CONNECTION IN AN URBAN SETTING

Qualitative research was the methodology adopted for this project to investigate the general knowledge of select members of a traditional church before and after effective training in leadership. John W. Creswell, in his book entitled *Research Design Qualitative, Quantitative and mixed Methods Approaches,* suggested the use of Qualitative research in the following ways: open ended questions, emerging approaches, text, or image data.[135] It would include testing an experimental group to measure whether or not any significant progress was made in their knowledge about church leadership. The experimental group consisted of nine persons who held a leadership position and three who did not at the time of the project. The study was done at an urban church in Newport News, Virginia. The experimental group was asked to be a part of this six week project that focused on equipping leaders to lead others in the 21st century. I discovered that many of the leaders and non-leaders in the focus group were excited

---

[135] John W. Creswell, *Research Design Qualitative, Quantitative and Mixed Methods Approaches,* Second edition (Thousand Oaks, Sage Publications, 2003), 19.

about the project, the transformation and information that it would bring. A pre and post-test was administered for the purpose of evaluating the results. A strategy was adopted for data collection during each session to determine the effectiveness.

Statement of the Problem

It is my opinion that the leadership of the church had experienced many challenges and changes. The church expressed its concerns regarding the lack of effective leadership in the church, the changes that were taking place and the conflict that the changes were causing. Most of the leadership, at that time, was seasoned and had been serving in positions for years. There was a need to equip the leaders in the church to do ministry and missions. Some in the church expressed their desire to be trained for leadership. Therefore, a leadership model was designed to strengthen the leadership of the church by equipping leaders to lead others and become more effective leaders in the 21st century.

Hypothesis

Twelve key leaders can be transformed by effective training, teaching and preaching. This transformation will in turn produce more effective leaders. The hypothesis will be tested with the use of surveys, group assessments and oral and written tests.

Intervention (Description of Ministry Project)

The purpose of this strategic study was to develop the effectiveness of the leadership for an urban church in Newport News, Virginia. The intervention consisted of four major components:
(a). Pre-test of the basic line knowledge of the leaders understanding of leadership
(b). Leaders' assessment tool to discover their leadership style
(c). Observation of leaders during training sessions to determine if they comprehended the material
(d). Post-test of the basic line knowledge of the leaders understanding of leadership at the end of the project.

At this stage in the research, the leadership will be defined as "the twelve." The qualitative research method was chosen to prove that by training "the twelve," they can become more effective in leading others in the 21st century. The project consisted of six weeks of training, teaching, and preaching about leadership. The leadership model was based on the models presented in chapter three. A series of five sermons on the topic, *"Equipping Leaders to Lead Others: A Leadership Paradigm for the Twenty First Century"*, were delivered over a five week period and a five week Bible study series. In addition, there were three training sessions on administrative skills, discovering your leadership style, and conflict resolution.

The first paradigm of change was the training and equipping "the twelve" to deal with administrative skills. They were taught the major points of the prescription for collaboration of leadership, and the process of connections and systems presented by Charles Tidwell in his book *Church Administration Effective Leadership for Ministry*.

Next, they were taught how to prepare agendas and the components that should be on the agenda such as: The purpose of the meeting, preparing an opening statement, prayer, review of last meeting and action items, content of the desired outcome, closing, review action steps/who/time, next agenda, thanks/ celebration recognition, and joys and concerns and prayers. Then, they were taught ministry planning. A template was used to evaluate how to plan to achieve a desired outcome that will help to bring about transformation in the lives of participants (discipleship). Finally, they were taught how to do strategic planning and keep up with accomplishments. A template outlined significant accomplishments, top opportunity areas, key learning, and next steps.

The second paradigm of change was the training and equipping "the twelve" to recognize their leadership style. The instrument used was the "Behavior Individuality Traits Profile." This profile helped the leader discover his or her particular style. There were four categories: commander, coach, counselor, and conductor. In discovering their unique style of leadership, they could be more effective in leading others to discover theirs. In the sermon series, we dealt with some of these styles.

The third paradigm of change involved equipping "the twelve" with the tools on conflict resolution. They were taught how to plan an interpersonal conflict resolution session. Before the resolution session, they were to consider the following questions: (1) What is the desired outcome on this meeting? What is your goal for the relationship/situation, and how would you like to be perceived at the end of the session? (2) What are the potential causes of the conflict? What did each party contribute to the conflict? (3) How do the other people involved perceive the conflict? (4) How might the other people respond to this meeting? How might they feel? What might they say? How could you respond to their feelings/comments? During the meeting, these steps were to be followed: (1) Establish rapport and ground rules. Set the stage for openness, respect, and mutually satisfactory problem-solving (not criticism). (2) Describe the conflict. Be objective and specific. (3) Ask others to share their perspectives. Listen to what they have to say without assuming you already have all the information you need. (4) Identify the points of agreement and disagreement. (5) Solicit potential solutions from the parties involved. If you are one of the parties, offer your own suggestions. (6) Evaluate the options. Which ones will satisfy all people involved? Remind everyone that the goal is mutual satisfaction, not a victory for one side, and that everyone might have to compromise. (7) Select an option and develop a plan of action. Be specific about who will do what and by when. (8) End the meeting with expressions of appreciation for each person's participation and contribution to the process. In addition, "the twelve" were taught how to lead through transition (change). A template helped them prepare for leading a group through an upcoming change. In the sermon series, we dealt with areas of change and the results of change.

Research Design

The purpose of this experimental study was to test the theory that leaders can be equipped to lead others to do effective ministry. The study also sought to show the leader his or her weaknesses and strengths and expose the leaders to three major areas that would help them bring about meaningful change in the church. It was designed to expose the twelve key leaders to administrative skills, styles of leadership, and conflict resolution.

The study was designed to evaluate the following questions:

1. **Are you familiar with the basic administrative skills in leading a ministry?**

2. **What are your strengths/weaknesses in the ministry?**

3. **What is your attitude about change?**

4. **Do you know your particular style of leadership?**

5. **Are you equipped to handle conflict management?**

6. What is the difference between interpersonal conflict and situational conflict?

Measurement

The measurement of the project was determined by a qualitative method using data triangulation. Data triangulation involves the use of different sources of data and information. I used surveys, group assessment, and oral and written tests to measure the effectiveness of the project.

Instrumentation

A pre-test and post-test were administered to determine the general knowledge of the leaders and the effectiveness of the project. The group was also given questions to answer after each sermon and bible study to test their understanding of the material. These instruments were vital in helping to determine the effectiveness of the project.

CHAPTER VI - THE "HOLY" CONNECTION

IN AN URBAN SETTING

Discussion Questions

1. What are the challenges and changes you would like to see happen in your context?

   _____
   _____
   _____
   _____
   _____
   _____

2. What is your hypothesis to change the situation?

   _____
   _____
   _____
   _____
   _____
   _____

3. Give a description of the ministry that you are involved in.

   _____
   _____
   _____
   _____
   _____

4. How will you handle the conflict that will come because of the changes you are making?

   _____
   _____
   _____
   _____
   _____
   _____

5. What does a resolution session look like to resolve the problem? What questions should be raised to resolve the conflict that may occur?

   _____
   _____
   _____
   _____
   _____
   _____

6. Are you familiar with the basic administrative skills in leading a ministry?

   _____
   _____
   _____
   _____
   _____
   _____

7. What are you strengths and weaknesses in the ministry?

8. What is your attitude about change?

9. Do you know your particular style of leadership?

10. Are you equipped to handle conflict management?

11. What is the difference between interpersonal conflict and situational conflict?

_____
_____
_____
_____
_____
_____

CHAPTER VII

THE CONCLUSION

As I reflect on this experience, it is an undeniable fact that no complete transformation of leaders can be done in the six week sessions. The transformation process only begins there but is an opportunity to raise and address concerns about the overall leadership in the church. "The twelve" were given the information for transformation and it appeared to be moving the leadership in the right direction. However, I realize that it will take time to bring about transformation and effective change.

In the beginning, I assumed that I had a broad understanding of leadership. However, by listening to the voices of those who had experience and wisdom on their side, I became aware of how much I did not know. This project has taken me to another level of understanding. I have grown with "the twelve" that I was leading.

I learned some beneficial lessons during this project. The first is that leadership is about empowering those around you to help you bear the load of leadership. The model that was developed was helpful in doing this. When observing how Moses and Jesus empowered those around them to do the work, it helped me to understand that he needed to rely upon other people to help bear the responsibilities that come with leadership. There must be a collaboration of leadership, processes, and systems. This method will enable the leader to be more effective. In developing leaders, I have built some relationships with people who have caught on to the vision and are running with it.

The second lesson learned is that change can bring on many challenges. When reflecting upon all the challenges that I have experienced in the ministry, it was because change was taking place. Conflict/challenges can be healthy. In teaching the lessons and preaching the sermons, I did not want to give the impression that it was okay to be in conflict but that conflict could help us to understand each other and find mutual ground. It also opens the door for dialogue.

The third lesson learned is that the church is open to new and creative ideas from leadership. When "the twelve" met, they were excited about the new methods and models of leadership that they were going to experience. They were open to the idea of teaching other leaders the information that was shared with them. They were instrumental in shaping my attitude about the leadership of the church because they were a part of the culture. They would often encourage me to keep a positive attitude about what God is going to do in the church. The leadership team was a broad spectrum of persons across the church. A few of them were educators, retirees, new members, young adult professionals and non- professionals. They opened my eyes to things that the church could be doing.

Finally, as I reflect on this project, it has sharpened my knowledge and awareness concerning leadership. It has helped me to become a better leader and pastor. I now have a model that can be shared with others who are interested in equipping their leaders for effective ministry. This model has strengthened my tools and enhanced my understanding about leadership and the different components that are involved in leadership.

SUMMARY AND CONCLUSION

In summary, I learned that it will take more time to bring about a meaningful change in the church. Although there was some change, it was not enough to bring about long term change.

During the study of this project, I had the opportunity to learn alongside "the twelve". As a teacher/pastor, I was confronted with many challenges and situations that needed the expertise of a well-rounded professional in the church and the community.

The expectations I have concerning the ministry are high. I have seen lives changed and transformed by teaching and preaching the different models presented in this book. It will take the help of the Holy Spirit to move and make people into what God has called them to be in the world in which we live. The church should be an agent of change in the community. God changes people and people change the community. I continue to believe that God is calling me to transform a generation (through leadership) that has been hurt and harmed by past experiences into a paradigm of a refreshing experience with God through serving the church and community at large. The church's journey was somewhat like my spiritual journey. It had experienced some great success and disappointments but I believe that God is calling the church to bring certainty in the midst of uncertainty and see the potential to push beyond the perils of life and maintain a sense of great joy.

ANSWER KEY

CHAPTER II - GOD, THE "HOLY" LIBERATOR

Fill in the blank

1. A theology of (**liberation**) must be the foundation of this God mandated experience because it will show us how God is liberating His people.

2. Church leaders must believe not only in the (**biblical**) and (**practical**) aspects of church work but they must believe it is ordained by God.

3. Church leaders both (**lay**) and (**clergy**) must have a level of theological training that is consistent with their leadership responsibility.

4. Leaders must keep in mind that (**liberation theology**) is at the center of Christian religion.

5. There can be no good (**Christian Theology**) if it is not connected with the downcast and underprivileged.

6. God was about (**liberating**) those who are on the bottom of the social order.

7. Leaders must keep in mind that the (**Exodus**) event was a part of God's liberation plan.

8. Leaders must realize that the exodus of the children of Israel is a (**perfect picture**) of a God who is the God of and for those who labor are heavy burdened.

9. It is through liberation that God uses leaders to deliver his people from the snares of being (**marginalized**)

11. It is the responsibility of total leadership in the church to (**aid**) and (**assist**) those who are marginalized by society in giving them the helping hand that they need.

GOD AS A LIBERATOR
Answer True or False

1. (**T**) God used a process to liberate them.
2. (**T**) God elected Israel to be His people.

3. **(F)** God appointed a leader by the name of Samuel in spite of his insufficiencies.
4. **(F)** God is at His worst when liberating those who are oppressed by the hand of the oppressor.
5. **(T)** In the history of God's revealed Word, the Bible indicates how very active God is in advocating for the poor and less fortunate because of His love for them.
6. **(F)** God is not concerned about the liberation of His people.
7. **(T)** Liberation is achieved through His process.
8. **(T)** God always identifies with the oppressed.
9. **(T)** The oppressed are connected with a God who sees them in their oppressive condition and delivers them from them all.
10. **(F)** Moses felt sufficient to lead the children of Israel.
11. **(T)** If theology is going to be relevant, it must speak to the ills of community.
12. **(T)** Jesus started his ministry dealing with the forces that had God's people in oppression.
13. **(F)** His public ministry focused on those who were high class and the upper-class.

14. **(F)** His messages and life was about himself and nobody else.
15. **(T)** His religion is a clear response to the oppression and suffering of his people.
16. **(T)** He had many followers but he equipped the twelve to turn the world upside-down to institute change in a world that resisted change.
17. **(T)** He taught and equipped the twelve concerning liberation.
18. **(T)** Leaders should always consider the Biblical hermeneutic concerning liberation.
19. **(T)** It is vital that one look at the Bible for motifs that will help aid in understanding the Bible in human liberation.
20. **(T)** Human liberation is not for people of color only, but for persons who find themselves oppressed by a culture of oppressors.

CHAPTER III - THE "HOLY" CONNECTION IN THE OLD TESTAMENT

Fill in the blank

1. The contemporary church is comprised of all kinds of (**leaders**).

2. The sad fact is that many leaders are (**unaware**) of the position that has been given to them.

3. Leadership in the local church is different from other (**sectors**) in our society.

4. The church is not an organization but an (**organism**) that lives and gives birth to helping hurting humanity.

5. The Old Testament model contends that (**Moses**) was the most important and significant leader in the life of Israel.

6. (**Moses**) was commissioned by God to lead God's people to a land flowing with milk and honey.

7. (**Moses**) had the courage to confront the many challenges of dealing with Pharaoh, although he felt insufficient.

8. Moses was committed to God and offered (**hope**) in spite of contention in the crowd.

9. Moses was confident that God would establish his (**leadership**).

10. God instructed Moses to take off his (**shoes**) as a sign of reverence.

CHAPTER IV - THE "HOLY" CONNECTION IN THE NEW TESTAMENT

Fill in the blank

1. The discussion of leadership concerning the contemporary church must being with (**Jesus Christ**) — who stated that "thou art Peter and upon this rock I will build my church."

2. Jesus achieved his mission by (**preaching, teaching, healing,** and **giving**) of himself.

3. Jesus preached about (**the Kingdom of God**).

4. The English phrase (**Kingdom of God**) refers primarily to the act or process of ruling, equality or privilege that distinguishes a king or other ruler.

5. Jesus is pictured using the Kingdom of God in four major ways:

- To express the Kingdoms preeminence
- To defend his personal authority to represent the Kingdom and divine will
- To imply the nature of his self-awareness the view he holds about his relationship with God and the meaning of his kingship
- To proclaim the kingdom's radical demand for total commitment

6. Throughout the (**synoptic gospels**) the Kingdom of God appears to dominate the message of Jesus.

7. (**Preaching**) that is transformative will focus on the Kingdom of God.

8. Jesus achieved his mission by (**teaching**).

9. Jesus allowed his teaching to impact the (**masses**) versus the (**masses**) impacting him.

10. Jesus disciples did not focus on learning his words, they focused on learning his (**lifestyle**).

Answer True or False

1. (**T**) It is through teaching that we equip the saints for ministry.
2. (**T**) The importance of teaching will help the believer to understand the commands that Jesus has left for us to do.

3. **(F)** Jesus was a traditional healer who was interested in healing both ills and diseases for charge.

4. **(T)** Diseases refer to what is physically wrong with a person while ills refer to a social consciousness of the disease, such as isolation, depression, etc.

5. **(T)** The mind is at peace once it has been taught the Word of God.

6. **(T)** As a leader, Jesus was a perfect model for all to follow.

7. **(T)** Christ lesson on greatness teaches us that the one who is the least is the servant.

8. **(T)** In order to be a great leader servants first must not be self-serving.

9. **(T)** Jesus took on menial tasks and stooped to do the jobs that no one else would do.

10. **(T)** A great example of the servant spirit that Jesus presented to his followers can be seen during the Passover prior to him being crucified; Jesus washed their feet.

CHAPTER V - THE "HOLY" CONNECTION
Answer True or False.

1. **(T)** Historically church fathers have seen the need for leadership in the church.
2. **(T)** There can be no church community without a leader or team leader.
3. **(F)** Weak leadership has been the key to developing and maintaining a healthy church.
4. **(F)** Training leaders has to be an one time process.
5. **(F)** It's okay to assume you know and don't know, nobody will find out.
6. **(T)** The pew is crying out for leadership.
7. **(T)** The leader in a context must see in people greatness even though they cannot see it.
8. **(F)** Historically leadership training was not important for leaders to develop and maintain a level of training to keep leaders on task and relevant in their particular context.
9. **(T)** The position of promise and possibility is a place designated by God.
10. **(F)** It is imperative that leaders see the bad in people they are leading.

NOTES

SUPPORTING LITERATURE TO UNDERSTAND THE "HOLY"

This literature is paramount to equipping leaders for the twenty first century. In exploring the problem of ineffective leadership in the church, it is imperative that one view the ideologies and trends of thought of different authors. It is my belief that every leader must be exposed to a wide view concerning leadership. This literature review will cover a broad spectrum of historical, theological, and biblical authors and editors who will challenge and enlighten the reader to a broader understanding of leadership.

HISTORICAL PERSPECTIVE

These authors and editors help me support the historical foundation of this book. Some of the authors are not quoted in this book; however they laid the foundation for me to understand the concept of leadership in a broader sense.

In Ken Blanchard and Phil Hodges book *The Servant Leader,* they deal with the servant leader model concerning leadership. It contends that Jesus was a servant leader for those in whom he lead. It gives a good historical perspective concerning leadership.

In Dalton Conley's book *Being Black, Living in the Red,* he deals with race, wealth, and social policy in America. Conley's persuasive analysis, the locus of current racial inequality resides in class and property relations, not in the labor market. It compares the wealth of the black-white differential. It also represents contributions to the race-class debate in the past two decades. Although not quoted, he helped me understand the racial divide in this century and its meaning to the black church.

In Gwen Ellis' book *God's Word of Life for Leaders,* she offers a devotion book about leadership and the biblical models concerning leadership. It is an excellent book for spiritual growth for leaders.

In Carol Cartmill and Yvonne Gentile's book *Leadership Essentials,* they deal with the essentials concerning leadership and the different models that the Bible presents. It shows a model about equipping the saints for service.

In Geoffrey V. Guns' book *Setting the House in Order: A Guide for Leading Change in the Local Church,* he shares a guide for leading change in the local church. It deals with how the church can bring about meaningful change with strong leadership.

In John Hendrix and Lloyd Householder's book *The Equipping of Disciples: Biblical Models of a Church's Training Ministry,* they take a serious look at discipleship and how it was a great concern for Jesus, Paul, and others during the New Testament era. Although not quoted, it helped me understand discipleship with greater clarity.

In Jim Herrington, Mike Bonem, James H. Furr book *Leading Congregational Change: A Practical Guide for the Transformational Journey,* they deal with leading change in a congregational setting. It is a practical guide for leading those who desire to bring about change in a traditional church setting.

In John Jackson and Lorraine Bosse'-Smith's book *Leveraging Your Leadership Style,* they contend that leadership is an art, not a science. The early stages of the twenty-first century, we are learning that leadership is a human endeavor that demands skills and grace not easily learned in educational, corporate, or seminar settings. This is in the appendix where the leader discovers his leadership style from a historical perspective.

In John Maxwell's book *The 21 Irrefutable Laws of Leadership,* he offers a variety of leadership laws that will enable the leader to move from one stage to the next. He points out how the leader must know his or her place in leadership.

Emmanuel L. McCall edited of the book *The Black Christian Experience.* He purposes that the book has a twofold meaning: (1) provide information to white Christians about the black church and (2) "help black Baptists understand and appreciate their heritage, hoping that by doing so they could accentuate the positive and eliminate negative." These eight writers speak plainly about beliefs and practices as they know them in black Baptist churches in the North and South. They share frustrations and hopes, limitations and dreams, and many problems and devotions of black believers. Although I did not quote him, it was helpful in understanding the black church experience.

In Lora-Ellen McKinney's book *Christian Education in the African American Church: A Guide for Teaching Truth,* she provides both theoretical and practical guidance in virtually all areas of Christian education in the African American church. She explores learning styles of young children, pre-adolescents, adolescents, and adults, including information on teaching individuals with special needs. Although I did not quote her, it was helpful in understanding different learning styles.

Wayne Meeks edited a book, *The New Testament in Its Social Environment: Stambaugh and Balch,* that is a discussion of the political, religious, economic, and social features of Palestine, and the cities of the Roman Empire. It synthesized the result of recent scholarly work to help the reader understand the relationship between the earliest Christians and the world around them. Stambaugh and Balch lived in that Roman world, and they shared many of its perceptions. Although not quoted, it helped me to understand the Roman world and its views on leadership.

In Thomas C. Oden's book *How Africa Shaped the Christian Mind: Rediscovering the African Seedbed of Western Christianity,* he deals with how Africa played a decisive role in the formation of Christian culture. Decisive intellectual achievement of Christianity was explored and understood first in Africa before they were recognized in Europe and a millennium before they found their way to North America. Christianity has a much longer history than its Western or European expressions. The profound ways African teachers have shaped world Christianity have never been adequately studied or acknowledged, either in the global North or South. Although not quoted, it helped me in understanding the historical perspective concerning how Africa helped shape the western world view about Christianity and leadership.

In E. Stanley Ott's book *Transform Your Church with Ministry Teams,* he discusses the power of the ministry-team concept, the issues involved in transitioning a church to a team-based approach, elements involved in beginning a ministry team, and the specifics of ministry-team life. Although not quoted, it was taught during the leadership training session.

In David Ramey's book *Empowering the Leaders,* he deals with how the leader should empower those around him or her to bring about effective leadership. It is a good book for equipping the leaders for the ministry. It supported the main concept of equipping those around you for effective ministry. It helped me to understand the importance of equipping leaders to equip others.

In Warren H. Stewart's Sr. book *Interpreting God's Word in Black Preaching,* he combined marvelous new work in hermeneutics with an amazingly accurate and deeply sensitive familiarity with the black preaching tradition. He writes about black heroes (preachers and their hermeneutical approach) of the faith. He had also written glowing accounts of worship in the black Brooklyn Baptist congregation where he was a member and Gardner C. Taylor was the pastor. Although not quoted, it offered a gem of information to the project especially from a historical perspective.

In Charles A. Tidwell's book *Church Administration: Effective Leadership for Ministry*, he deals with the development of a theory which includes the major elements of church administration and in terms of it functions. He also dealt with the leadership models of Jethro-Moses and Jesus.

In Stan Toler and Alan Nelson's book *The Five Star Church,* they offered a contemporary approach to ministry. It assists church leaders in understanding, in a contemporary tell-it-like-it-is style, how to build balanced ministries in every area of New Testament responsibilities. Although not quoted, it helped me to understand another contemporary approach to ministry.

In Lovett H. Weems book *Church Leadership: Vision Team Culture and Integrity,* she offers an interactive approach to leadership recognizing the importance of the relationship between leaders and followers. Leadership does not exist within a person; it resides in the relationship between persons. Leaders are defined by the power their followers lend them.

Followers, in turn, are empowered by leaders to do more than they ever imagined (13). The task of leadership is positive change. Leaders inspire others to their best efforts in order to do better; to attain higher purposes. Leaders are not satisfied with the status quo. They are idealist who believe that things can be better; utopians who dream of perfection. Leaders, therefore, must be change masters. They must understand how to create and guide innovation (11).

BIBLICAL PERSPECTIVE

These authors and editors assisted in the biblical foundation of this book. Although some authors are not quoted, they laid the foundation for understanding the elasticity of the concept of leadership.

In Michael Coogan's book *The Oxford History of the Biblical World,* he offers leading scholars compelling glimpses into the biblical world, the world in which prophets, poets, sages, and historians created the Bible. This book offers scholarship, and in chronologically ordered chapters, presents the reader with an integrated study of the history, art, architecture, languages, literatures, and religion of biblical Israel and early Judaism and Christianity in their larger cultural context. (2)

In Leroy Eims' book *Be the Leader you were Meant to be: Biblical Principles of Leadership,* he deals with leadership. He writes that we must be certain concerning the call to leadership. When one is asked to serve in one way or another, make certain that God has ordained it. Don't budge an inch in either direction—either yes or no—until you have determined the will of God in the matter.

In James Freeman's book *Manners & Customs of the Bible,* he goes through the Bible, explaining many customs practiced in the Bible times. It is not difficult to understand, and it is also filled with many helpful illustrations.

In Geoffrey Guns' book *Spiritual Leadership: A Guide to Developing Spiritual Leaders in the Church,* he asserts that the church, being a spiritual organism is called into being by God to achieve the purposes of God in the world. Therefore, those who lead are called by God to fulfill God's purpose and not their own agenda.

In Stephen L. Harris' book *The New Testament: A Student's Introduction 3rd ed.,* he deals with various theological positions and scholars from various points of view. He shows how liberation fits into the scheme of the God human experience.

In William R. Herzog's II book, *Prophet and Teacher: An Introduction to the Historical Jesus,* he deals with the historical facts concerning Jesus. It offers the reader insights on Jesus as a prophet and teacher.

In Floyd Massey Jr. and Samuel Berry McKinney's book, *Church Administration in the Black Perspective,* they provided a guideline for developing effective organization of church boards and committees as well as the overall church administrative structure based on the experiences of the African American Christian community. The text also explores how the African heritage and slave experiences have molded traditions that are significant in modern black church life. Although not quoted, this book assisted in understanding church administration from a black perspective.

In Tom Sine's book, *Taking Discipleship Seriously: a Radical Biblical Approach,* he takes a serious look a discipleship and how it strengthens the believer. It offers a strong biblical approach to leadership. Although not quoted, it helped me to understand the importance of discipleship training.

In John F. Walvoord and Roy B. Zuck's commentary *The Bible Knowledge Commentary: An Exposition of the Scriptures,* they deal with the interpretation of various books of the Bible. It is very contemporary in its discussion concerning biblical passages.

In Warren W. Wiersbe's book, *Wiersbe's Expository Outlines on the Old Testament,* he outlines the Old Testament in narrative form. It gives a vivid look at the Old Testament from a contemporary perspective. The outlines are very detailed and insightful due to its narrative genre.

THEOLOGICAL PERSPECTIVE

These authors and editors assisted in supporting the theological foundation of this book.

In James Cones' book, *A Black Theology of Liberation,* he deals with liberation theology. He believes that it is a rational study of the being of God in the world in light of the existential situation of an oppressed community, relating the forces of liberation to the essence of the gospel, which is Jesus Christ.

In James H. Evans' Jr. book, *We Have Been Believers,* he seeks to overcome the chasm between church practice and theological reflection, Evans situates theology squarely in the nexus of faith with freedom. It shares monumental theological arguments concerning liberation theology.

In David Ford's book, *The Modern Theologians: An Introduction to Christian Theology in the Twentieth Century*, he introduces the thoughts of the many leading twentieth-century Christian theologians, and movements in theology.

In Shirley C. Guthrie's book, *Christian Doctrine: Revised Edition,* she presents a book that is grounded in scripture, conversant with the reformed confessions and tradition, and remarkably relevant to the daily experience of the world. It offers help in understanding the Christian faith.

In Joseph H. Johnson's book, *Proclamation Theology,* he deals adequately with black theology. He argues the theological differences between James Cone and other theologians. Johnson provides this material to compare and contrast the difference in Cone, Barth, Bultman and Mitchell to name a few.

In Cleophus J. Larue's ed., book, *Power in the Pulpit: How America's Most Effective Black Preachers Prepare Their Sermons,* the writers were encouraged to pursue their own unique method of preparation. They were asked to reflect on and bring to conscious formation the methodological process they engage in each week. They were not privy to one another's work and were given the freedom to pursue their own particular take on the process.

In Richard Lischer's ed. book, *The Company of Preachers: Wisdom on Preaching, Augustine to the Present,* he deals with the voices that constitutes the church's homiletically tradition. It is arranged in seven divisions with between six and eleven selections under each division. There is a brief introduction to each selection and an attempt to maintain a conversation between the positions represented in the various selections. It was helpful in understanding the church's homiletically tradition and its theology.

In Leon Morris' book, *New Testament Theology*, he looks at what the New Testament authors meant. This is not an academic exercise, but a necessary prelude to our understanding of what their writing means for us today. It takes a fresh look liberation theology.

In Donald Musser, and Joseph L. Price's book, *A New Handbook of Christian Theologians,* they discuss human liberation yet asserting Womanist theologians who stated that "though they believe in the Bible, the Bible has historically served as a tool of oppression against women and ethnic and sexual minorities."

In J. Deotis Roberts' book, *Africentric Christianity: a Theological Appraisal for Ministry,* he points out that the history of Israel and the New Testament description of the historical Jesus reveal that God is identified with Israel because it is an oppressed community. The resurrection of Jesus means that all oppressed peoples become his people.

In David Smith's book, A *Handbook of Contemporary Theology,* he claims that liberation must be understood in its totality as removal of all which keeps the African in bondage, and all that makes him less than God intended him to be. The idea is that Jesus has the power to liberate from fear, illness, and evil, as well as oppression, racism, and exploitation.

In Edward L. Smith's book, *The Doctrine of Providence & Revelation: an Introduction to Philosophy and Theology,* he points out that Israel was the first elect, and divine election also encompassed the Gentiles. A remnant remains in every group that God has chosen depicting God's righteousness.

In Terry Thomas' handout, *An Exploration into the Task of Leadership,* lecture notes from cluster group, he offers a helpful guide for leaders to explore the task of leadership. It is impregnated with usable insights that will awaken the leadership style in leaders. It holds rich theology, biblical and historical information to aid the leader in understanding leadership roles.

In Owen C. Thomas and Ellen K. Wondra's book, *Introduction to Theology,* they deal with the exodus from Israel, Jesus' proclamation of the kingdom of God and his ministry, along with his death and resurrection, as key biblical events. Liberation entails two things: the thorough transformation of oppressive socioeconomic, political, and cultural systems into systems that promote the well-being and just treatment of all persons; and the coming into full humanity and dignity of those who have been oppressed, marginalized, or subjugated. These two aspects must be achieved together; one does not precede the other.

In Cornel West's book, *Race Matters,* he points out that "quality leadership is neither the product of one great individual nor the result of odd historical accidents. Rather, it comes from deeply bred traditions and communities that shape and mold talented and gifted persons. Without a vibrant tradition of resistance passed on to new generations, there can be no nurturing of a collective and critical consciousness — only professional conscientiousness survives." (56)

In Gustavo Gutierrez's book, *We Drink From Our Own Wells: The Spiritual Journey of A People*, he looks at the theology of Latin America and its relation to liberation theology. He points out that liberation theology was birthed in Latin America. It hails from the wells of our own experiences as we relentlessly pursue liberation.

BIBLIOGRAPHY

Blanchard, Ken and Phil Hodges, *The Servant Leader*. Nashville, TN: J. Countryman, 2003.

Blount, K. Brian., *Can I Get a Witness*. Louisville: Westminster John Knox Press, 2005.

Blue, Ken., *Healing Spiritual Abuse: How to Break Free from Bad Church Experiences*. Downers Grove, Illinois: Inter-Varsity Press, 1993.

Brueggermann, Walter, *The Creative Word,* Philadelphia: Fortress Press, 1982.

Buttrick, David, *Homiletic- Moves and Structures*. Philadelphia: Fortress Press, 1987.

Cashman, Kevin, *Awakening the Leader Within*. Hoboken, New Jersey: John Wiley & Sons, Inc., 2003.

Cartmill, Carol and Yvonne Gentile., *Leadership Essentials*. Nashville, TN: Abingdon Press, 2006.

Cone, H. James., *A Black Theology of Liberation*. 20th *Anniversary Edition*. Maryknoll, New York: Orbis Books, 1999.

Cone, James M., *My Soul Looks Back*. Maryknoll, New York: Orbis Books, 1986.

Cones, James., *A Black Theology Of Liberation*. Maryknoll, NY: Orbis Books, 1990.

Conley, Dalton., *Being Black, Living in the Red*. Berkeley and Los Angeles, California: University of California Press, 1999.

Coogan, Michael D., *The Oxford History of the Biblical World*. Oxford: University Press, 1998.

Dash, I. N. Michael and Jonathan Jackson and Stephen C. Rasor., *Hidden Wholeness: An African American Spirituality for individuals and Communities*. Cleveland: United Church Press, 1997.

Edwards, O. C., *The History Of Preaching*. Nashville: Abington, 2004.

Ellingsen, Mark., *The Richness of Augustine; His Contextual & Pastoral Theology*. Louisville: Westminster John Know Press, 2005.

Eims, Leroy. *Be the Leader you were meant to be: Biblical Principles of Leadership*. Wheaton, Ill.: Victor Books, 1977.

Ellis, Gwen., *God's Word of Life for Leaders*. Grand Rapid, Michigan: Zondervan Publishing House, 1999.

Eslinger, Richard L., *The Web of Preaching: New Options in Homiletic Method*. Nashville: Abingdon Press, 2002.

Evans, Jr. James H., *We Have Been Believers.* Minneapolis: Fortress Press, 1992.

Fitts, Leroy. *A History of Black Baptists*. Nashville: Broadman Press, 1985.

Floyd-Thomas, Stacey and Juan Floyd-Thomas and Carol B. Duncan and Stephen G. Ray and Nancy Lynne Westfield., *Black Church Studies: An Introduction*. Nashville: Abingdon Press, 2007.

Fluker, Walter Earl and Catherine Tumber, eds., *A Strange Freedom; The Best of Howard Thurman on Religious Experience and Public Life*. Boston: Beacon Press, 1998.

Ford, David. *The Modern Theologians: An Introduction to Christian Theology in the Twentieth Century*. Malden, Massachusetts: Blackwell Publishers Ltd, 1997.

Freeman, James M., *Manners & Customs of the Bible.* New Kensington, PA: Whitaker House, 1996.

Gorman, J. Michael., *Apostle of the Crucified Lord*. Grand Rapids: William B. Eerdmans 7th Edition Publishing Company, 2004.

Guns, Geoffrey V., *Setting the House in Order: A Guide for Leading Change in the Local Church.* Virginia Beach, Virginia: Bright Hope Publishing Company, 2004.

Guns, Geoffrey V., *Spiritual Leadership: A Guide to Developing Spiritual Leaders in the Church* Lithonia, GA.: Orman Press, Inc., 2000.

Guthrie, Shirley C., *Christian Doctrine: Revised Edition* Louisville: Westminster/John Knox Press 1994.

Gutierrez, Gustavo. *We Drink Our Well.* Maryknoll, New York: Orbis Book, 1984.

Harris, Stephen L., *The New Testament: A Student's Introduction* 3rd *ed.* Mountain View, California: Mayfield Publishing Company, 1999.

Hendrix, John and Lloyd Householder eds., *The Equipping of Disciples: Biblical Models of a Church's Training Ministry.* Nashville, TN: Broadman Press, 1977.

Herrington, Jim, Mike Bonem, James H. Furr, *Leading Congregational Change: A Practical Guide for the Transformational Journey.* San Francisco, CA: Jossey- Bass, 2000.

Herzog II., William R., *Prophet and Teacher: An Introduction to the Historical Jesus.* Louisville, Kentucky: Westminster John Knox Press, 2005.

Jenkins, Philip., *The Next Christendom: The Coming of Global Christianity*. New York: Oxford University Press, 2007.

Jones, A. Clifford Sr., *From Proclamation to Practice.* Valley Forge: Judson Press, 1993.

Jones, Amos Jr., *Paul's Message of Freedom: What Does it Mean to the Black Church.* Valley Forge: Judson Press, 1984.

Joyner, D. Ronnie ., *Functioning as a Deaconess: A Ministry of Care.* Lithonia, Georgia: Orman Press, 2002.

Jackson, John and Lorraine Bosse'-Smith., *Leveraging Your Leadership Style.* Nashville: Abingdon Press, 2007.

Johnson, Joseph, *Proclamation Theology.* Shreveport, Louisiana: Fourth Episcopal District Press, 1977.

Larue, Cleophus J. ed. *Power in the Pulpit: How America's Most Effective Black Preachers Prepare Their Sermons.* Louisville: Westminster John Knox Press, 2002.

Lischer, Richard ed., *The Company of Preachers: Wisdom on Preaching, Augustine to the Present.* Grand Rapids: Williams B. Eerdmans Publishing Company, 2002.

Massey, Floyd Jr., and Samuel Berry McKinney., *Church Administration in the Black Perspective.* Valley Forge: Judson Press, 1976.

Massey, James E. *Aspect of My Pilgrimage,* Anderson, Indian: Anderson University Press, 2002.

Maxwell, John C., *The 21 Irrefutable Laws of Leadership.* Nashville, TN: Thomas Nelson, 1998.

McCall, Emmanuel L. *The Black Christian Experience.* Nashville: Broaden Press, 1972.

McClary., R. Oscar., *Marketplace Anointing: The Power of Godly Leadership in Secular Society.* Kearney, Nebraska: Morris Publishing, 2007.

McIntosh, L. Gary., *One Church, Four Generations: Understanding and Reaching All Ages in Your Church.* Grand Rapids: Baker Books, 2002.

McKinney, Lora-Ellen., *Christian Education in the African American Church: A Guide for Teaching Truth.* Valley Forge: Judson Press, 2003.

Meeks, Wayne A. ed., *The New Testament in Its Social Environment: Stambaugh and Balch.* Philadelphia: Westminster Press, 1986.

Mitchell, Henry H. and Emil M. Thomas., *Preaching for Black Self-Esteem.* Nashville: Abingdon Press, 1994.

Mitchell, Henry H., *Celebration and Experience in Preaching.* Nashville: Abingdon Press, 1990.

Morris, Leon., *New Testament Theology*. Grand Rapids: Zondervan, 1986.

Musser, Donald W., & Joseph L. Price, *A New Handbook of Christian Theologians*. Nashville: Abingdon Press. 1996.

Oden, Thomas C., *How Africa Shaped the Christian Mind: Rediscovering the Africa Seedbed of Western Christianity*. Downers Grove, Illinois: Inter-Varsity Press, 2007.

Ott, E. Stanley., *Transform Your Church with Ministry Teams*. Grand Rapides, Michigan: William B. Eerdmans Publishing Company, 2004.

Proctor, Samuel D., *How Shall They Hear?* Valley Forge, Pa.: Judson Press, 1992.

Pliens, J. David, *The Social Vision of the Hebrew Bible*. Louisville, Westminster: John Knox Press, 2001.

Ramey, David A., *Empowering the Leaders*. Kansas City, Missouri: Sheed & Ward, 1991.

Roberts, J. Deotis., *Africentric Christianity: A Theological Appraisal For Ministry*. Valley Forge: Judson Press, 2000.

Robinson, Haddon, *Biblical Preaching*. Grand Rapids, Michigan: Baker Book House, 1980.

Scazzero, Peter., *The Emotionally Healthy Church*. Grand Rapids: Zondervan, 2003.

Schein, H. Edgar., *Organizational Culture and Leadership*. 2nd Edition. San Francisco: Jossey-Bass Publishers, 1992.

Sine, Tom., *Taking Discipleship Seriously: a Radical Biblical Approach*. Valley Forge: Judson Press, 1985.

Smith, p. Donald., *Empowering Ministry: Ways to Grow in Effectiveness*. Louisville: Westminster John Knox Press, 1996.

Smith, David L., *A Handbook of Contemporary Theology*. Grand Rapids: Baker Books, 1992

Smith, Edward L., *The Doctrine of Providence & Revelation: An Introduction to Philosophy and Theology*. Riverdale, GA: The Research Center Press, 2001.

Stewart, Warren H. Sr., *Interpreting God's Word in Blacking Preaching*. Valley Forge: Judson Press, 1984.

Sutherland, Dave and Kirk Nowery., *The Thirty-Three Laws of Stewardship: Principles for a Life of True Fulfillment*. Camarillo, California: Spire Resources Incorporated, 2003.

Taylor, Edward L., *50 Years of Timeless Treasures- Gardner Taylor*. Valley Forge: Judson Press, 2003.

Thompson, B. George Jr., *Alligators in the Swap: Power, Ministry and Leadership*. Cleveland: The Pilgrim Press, 2005.

Thompson, B. George Jr., *How to Get Along with Your Church*. Cleveland: The Pilgrim Press, 2001.

Thompson, B. George Jr., *How to Get Along with Your Pastor*. Cleveland: The Pilgrim Press, 2006.

Thomas, Terry., *An Exploration into the Task of Leadership,* lecture notes from cluster group/Handout.

Thomas, Owen C. and Ellen K. Wondra., *Introduction to Theology.* Harrisburg, PA: Morehouse Publishing, 2002.

Toler, Stan and Alan Nelson., *The Five Star Church* Ventura, CA: Regal Books from Gospel Light, 1999.

Tidwell, A. Charles. *Church Administration: Effective Leadership for Ministry*. Nashville: Broadman & Holman Publishers, 1985.

Tiffany, C. Frederick and Sharon H. Ringe., *Biblical Interpretation: A Roadmap*. Nashville: Abingdon Press, 1996.

Toler, Stan and Alan Nelson., *The Five Star Church: Serving God and His People with Excellence.* Ventura, California: Regal Books, 1999.

Turabian, L. Kate., *A Manual for Writers of Research Papers, Theses, and Dissertations.* Chicago: The University of Chicago Press, 2007.

Tye, B. Karen., *The Basics of Christian Education.* Danvers, Massachusetts: Chalice Press, 2000.

Walker, H. John., *A Fresh Look at the New Testament Deacon*. Lithonia, Georgia: Orman Press, Incorporated, 2001.

Webb, Henry., *Deacons: Servant Models in the Church*. Nashville: Convention Press, 1980.

Welborn, L.L., *Paul, the Fool of Christ: A Study of First Corinthians 1-4 in the Comic-Philosophic Tradition*. New York: T & T Clark International, 2005.

Wimbush, L. Vincent., *African Americans and the Bible*. New York: The Continuum International Publishing Group Incorporated, 2000.

Walvoord, John F. and Zuck, Roy B., *The Bible Knowledge Commentary: An Exposition of the Scriptures.* Wheaton, IL: Victor Books, 1983.

Weems, Lovett H., *Church Leadership: Vision Team Culture and Integrity.* Nashville: Abingdon Press, 1993.

West, Cornel., *Race Matters.* New York: Vintage Books, 2001.

Wiersbe, Warren W. *Wiersbe's Expository Outlines on the Old Testament*. Wheaton, IL: Victor Books, 1993.

Order Information

To contact Dr. Dawkins for preaching, teaching or speaking engagements,

Call 864-918-0243

Please email: (rdawk@aol.com) or call for bulk orders

You may also order paperback books through Amazon.com

Visit Dr. Dawkins at:

Triumph Christian Center
5501 Huntington Avenue
Newport News, VA 23607

www.ingramcontent.com/pod-product-compliance
Lightning Source LLC
Chambersburg PA
CBHW050635300426
44112CB00012B/1814